TWENTIETH
CENTURY
WORLD
HISTORY

INDIA AND PAKISTAN
IN THE TWENTIETH CENTURY

RICHARD TAMES

86267

BATSFORD ACADEMIC AND EDUCATIONAL *LONDON*

CONTENTS

ACKNOWLEDGMENT

The Author and Publishers thank the following for their kind permission to reproduce copyright illustrations: Associated Press Ltd for figs 54, 55, 56; BBC Hulton Picture Library for figs 7, 8; Camera Press for figs 43, 44, 53; India Office Library and Records for figs 13, 17, 18, 19, 24, 28, 30; International Development Association for fig 46 (photograph by J.Breitenbach); the Mansell Collection for figs 9, 14, 16, 21, 22, 32, 34; Popperfoto for figs 3, 11, 12, 15, 20, 23, 25, 26, 27, 29, 31, 33, 37, 38, 42, 48, 49, 50, 51, 52, 57; John Topham Picture Library for fig 35; World Bank for fig 47 (photograph by Ray Witlin). Figs 1, 2, 4, 5, 6, 39, 40 and 45 are the property of the Author. The maps were drawn by Chartwell Illustrators. Thanks are also expressed to Peta Hambling for the picture research on this book.

First published 1981
Second impression 1984
© Richard Tames 1981

ISBN 0 7134 3415 5

Printed and bound in Great Britain by Anchor/Brendon Ltd, Tiptree, Essex for the Publishers Batsford Academic and Educational, an imprint of B T Batsford Ltd, 4 Fitzhardinge Street, London W1H 0AH

INDIA: A CULTURE AND A CONTINENT

India is not a country but a continent. More than a million square miles in area, it embraces both deserts and jungles, some of the world's longest rivers and the world's highest mountain ranges. Most of its people live in villages, but it also contains, in Calcutta, Delhi, Bombay and Madras, some of the world's largest cities.

1   The Taj Mahal, a mausoleum built by Shah Jahan (1627-58) in memory of his wife, Mumtaz Mahal. Intricate marble inlay and elaborate formal gardens make it one of the world's architectural masterpieces.

2 Children today drive an ox to turn a "Persian wheel" to raise water for irrigation — as they did in the days of Shah Jahan, and long before.

In terms of area and population, India may far more reasonably be compared with Europe (including European Russia) than with any single country within it. Europe, in the modern sense, is the heir of Christendom and is divided between Catholic, Protestant and Orthodox traditions. Overlying this is the division between the capitalist west and the communist east. Since 1945 the democratic nations of western Europe have tried to create institutions which would enable them to act more effectively together. But continuing political disputes between the member states of the EEC show how difficult this can be. The diversity of languages spoken in Europe adds another layer of practical problems to be overcome in the quest for greater unity.

By comparing India with Europe as a whole, we can begin to understand why it is unhelpful to think of India as we tend to think of a "normal" country — one in which everyone speaks the same language and accepts the same general pattern of beliefs and behaviour. We can begin to understand why India has adopted a federal form of government, why the various states are mostly based on language-groups,

and why religious distinctions still retain a political significance.

Diversity has long been India's most distinctive characteristic. The lives of her peoples are governed by two of the world's great religious traditions — Hinduism and Islam. Sikhism, Jainism and Christianity also all have millions of followers. Yet India proclaims itself to be a secular state, whose constitution favours the followers of no religion above any other.

More than eight hundred languages are spoken in India today. Many of these tongues are spoken by only a few thousand or even hundreds of tribal peoples. But languages like Telugu, Marathi and Tamil have tens of millions of speakers — that is, as many as Greek or Polish and far more than Dutch or Swedish. The Indian constitution recognizes fourteen official languages. And the language most generally understood among the educated class who govern India is English, the language of the former colonial power. English is widely used, therefore, in the universities and law courts and in commerce and industry.

What, then, does it mean to be an Indian? An Indian may be a Punjabi-speaking, illiterate

3 Sikh, Hindu and Muslim boys in an open-air class. The wall painting shows a ceremonial procession customary in Rajasthan at the time of a wedding.

4 Election posters in English and an advertisement for a language school show the continuing importance of the English language. The other language shown is Hindi, which is widely spoken in northern and central India.

Muslim peasant farmer or an English-educated, Bengali-speaking lawyer with no particular religion at all. An Indian may be an elderly and pious widow living in a medium-sized city or an eager young school-girl about to leave her native village. As the English novelist E.M. Forster once wrote, "there is no such thing as a 'general Indian'."

Economically also, India exhibits great diversity. India has 150 million cows and the world's largest steel mill. India is a nuclear power and a major manufacturer of motor cars and radios, and yet 80 per cent of the people depend on the land for their living.

Economic diversity is reflected in an extremely uneven distribution of wealth. There is a numerically small, but influential and very wealthy upper class of politicians, industrialists, former princes and current film stars. There is a rapidly growing urban middle class of civil servants and professional men. In the countryside there are, in many villages, landowners with medium-sized holdings who dominate the affairs of their local communities. And while the bulk of the population are still impoverished agricultural workers, it must not be forgotten that there is a new class of factory workers as well. But they are far out-numbered by the 40 million "tribals", many of whom still live, remote from the cities or great cultivated plains and river valleys, in jungles and mountain areas, following a way of life that is only now beginning to change under the impact of modern technology and communications and the concern of the Indian government that they should, in due course, play their full part in the nation's life.

If there is one institution, however, whose significance all Indians recognize, it is caste. Caste cannot be explained in a few words. Although it is often referred to as a "system", in practice it admits of too many variations to deserve the name. Caste has dominated Indian society for three thousand years. Its origins are obscure, but the main principles of its operation can be summarized as follows:

(a) Indians are born into a caste. Recruitment is hereditary.
(b) Castes are distinguished from one another to a certain extent by their occupations and to a much greater extent by patterns of marriage and ritual. Caste members marry members of the same caste, and may be "polluted" by various forms of contact (through eating, washing, etc) with members of different castes.
(c) The existence of caste as a social tradi-

tion is bound up with Hinduism as a religious tradition. Nevertheless, non-Hindu groups are also expected to find a place in the overall hierarchy of castes.

(d) Standing outside the hierarchy of castes are the "untouchables", some 90 million whose very shadow is regarded as polluting by caste Hindus. Among the poorest of the poor, largely illiterate, often forced to live apart from other villagers, the untouchables were re-named "harijans" — "children of God" — by Gandhi. He tried to raise their status and, following this example, the Indian government has abolished the legal status of "untouchables" and tried to improve their condition through preferential treatment in education and employment. Nevertheless, discrimination persists, and untouchables attempting to use the same wells or temples as their fellow villagers are often met with violence. In an attempt to improve their status, many untouchables have renounced Hinduism and converted to Christianity or Buddhism. Until recently Buddhism seemed almost to have died out in the land of its birth. The 1951 census recorded only 181,000 Buddhists in India. But by 1961 there were 3,300,000, most of them recent converts in Maharashtra, following the example of Dr B.R. Ambedkar, the untouchables' national leader.

All societies bear the marks of continuity and change. But in India the continuities stretch back for three thousand years, and the changes are as rapid as can be found in any of the world's developing nations. New diversities of experience are added to the old distinctions of birth and background. The unity of modern India springs not so much from a memory of the ancient past or from a common struggle in the present as from the experience of British rule and the reaction that it created. Many times in its history India has been ruled by alien conquerors and has accepted their rule with little protest. What made British rule different was that it introduced to India new ideas and new technologies and contacts with a wider world. It is no coincidence that the movement for Indian national unity and independence began in Bengal, the area which first came under British influence and remained so the longest, nor that the movement's earliest leaders were not Brahmin priests, the guardians of India's ancient Hindu heritage, but western-educated lawyers, journalists and officials, whose learning and occupations were themselves the products of colonial rule. Because their countrymen were dispersed over such a wide area and divided by differences of caste, language and religion, the task that faced the early nationalists, of making Indians see themselves as members of a single nation, was vast indeed. This book is largely concerned with the ways in which that task was accomplished.

YOUNG HISTORIAN

A
1 In what ways is India more like the continent of Europe as a whole than like any one state within it?
2 Make a summary of the main differences between Hinduism and Islam. Which do you think are the most important?
3 Why is caste so important? Why has it persisted for so long?
4 What is nationalism? Why is it so important in the modern world?
5 Explain the meaning of (a) federal, (b) secular, (c) hereditary, (d) hierarchy, (e) "untouchable".

B

Imagine you are organizing a tour of India, intended to show the visitor something of every important aspect of the Indian peoples' ways of life. Make out an itinerary of the visits you would want him or her to make. (See also page 74 — 81.)

What different methods of travel would you use for each stage of the journey?

C

Suppose you could meet three different sorts of people from India. Whom would you choose to meet? Explain your choice and make up three questions you would like to ask them.

D

Draw a map of India and mark in the main cities, rivers and mountainous areas. Draw another map and mark in where each of the main languages is spoken.

RAJ

THE EAST INDIA COMPANY

Direct British rule in India lasted for only ninety years. Before 1857 the commerce and politics of India were largely controlled by the merchants and officials of the London-based East India Company. Their interest in the continent had begun in the early seventeenth century, when the fabulous wealth of the Mughal empire tempted Englishmen to sail halfway round the world to trade for rare spices, fine muslins and delicately wrought

metalwares. Involvement in Indian trade led to involvement in Indian wars as the Mughal empire broke up. By 1818 the East India Company, its army and administrators had become the dominant power in the sub-continent. The last Mughal emperors were rulers in name only.

During the 1820s and 1830s the British in India changed their former policy of not intervening in the everyday life of the people and began to suppress what they regarded as evil customs, such as the burning of widows and the killing of female infants. They also introduced western education and western laws and began to build railways into the interior of the country. Some Indians were impressed by the civilization of the west, but many resented these "reforms" as an attack on India's traditional way of life.

THE MUTINY

When a section of the East India Company's army mutinied in 1857, there was a widespread rising in North India against British rule. How-

◄ 7 The storming of Delhi, 1857. Indian units were never again entrusted with artillery.

8 Aftermath of revolt, 1857 — the Kashmir Gate, Delhi where the British made their first break-through.

"NEW CROWNS FOR OLD ONES!"

(ALADDIN *adapted.*)

9 Disraeli creates Victoria "Empress of India". (*Punch* cartoon of 1876).

ever, most of the army stayed loyal to the British, and, because the rebels had no clear plan of action, they were defeated. As a result of the rising, the powers of government in India were transferred by Act of Parliament from the East India Company to the British Crown itself. The moral that Englishmen drew from the experience of what they called "The Mutiny" was that British rule in India must be firm, vigilant against opposition, and careful not to introduce changes too rapidly, lest they provoke public disorder.

DIRECT BRITISH RULE

By 1900 direct British rule in India had reached its halfway mark, though anyone predicting that it would end within fifty years would certainly have been met with complete astonishment. British rule seemed not only secure. To the British, at least, it seemed almost inevitable. At the turn of the century Sir John Strachey, a leading British official, wrote:

> We cannot foresee the time in which the cessation of our rule would not be the signal for universal anarchy and ruin . . . the only hope for India is the long continuance of the benevolent but strong government of Englishmen.

British rule in India had led to the construction of the world's most extensive railway network, the introduction of a modern postal and telegraph system, the imposition of order

10   British India, 1857-1947.

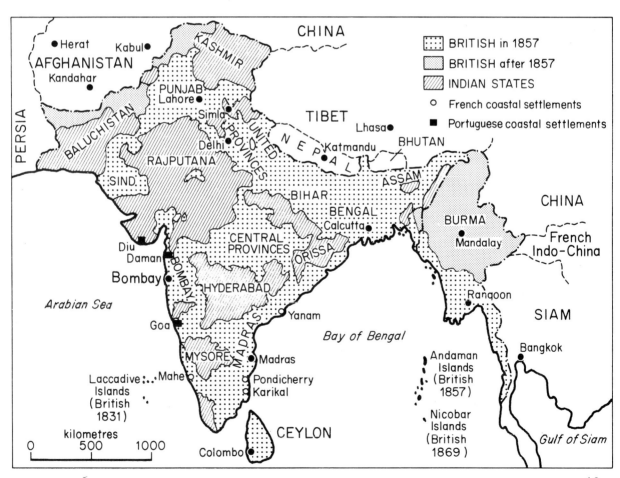

in frontier areas, and the creation of a 40,000-mile network of irrigation canals which brought into cultivation some 20 million acres of land. These immense accomplishments were largely the work of the Indian Civil Service (ICS), an elite of some 5,000 carefully selected Englishmen, assisted by a growing clerical class of western-educated Indians and Anglo-Indians and backed by a powerful and efficient army of 250,000 men, paid for out of Indian taxes.

It is important to remember that only about half of India was under direct British rule; the rest was still in the hands of some six hundred native princes whose kingdoms ranged in size from half the size of England itself to smaller than an English county. These native rulers were obliged to accept British advisers and were usually honoured to accept British titles and decorations. Although the British retained the right to intervene in the affairs of princely states in the event of serious misgovernment, they rarely interfered in the day-to-day running of affairs. The external relations of the princely states were controlled by the British, but many rulers still kept up their own armies. Some of the princes were fabulously wealthy by any standards. Nearly all were considerably wealthier than their subjects, whose welfare they were largely free to improve or not, as they chose. Some princes built railways, schools and hospitals. Others used their revenues to pay for their personal pleasures. On the whole, so long as the princes did not challenge British rule, the British were content to exhort and encourage rather than warn or chide them.

For the Indian villager, British rule meant obedience to the orders and decisions of the district officer, a young man from a far country, who was the local representative of a large and complex hierarchy of officials, stretching up through the provincial government to the Viceroy and ultimately to the Secretary of State for India who sat in the British cabinet. The duties of a district officer were varied and demanding: everything, in the words of one of them, "from vaccination to education; from warding off a famine to counting the blankets of convicts in his jail; from taking a census to feeding an army on the march". His main tasks, however, were the collection of taxes,

the settlement of disputes and the promotion of improvements in agriculture and public health.

Far above the district officer stood the glittering figure of the Viceroy, resident in Calcutta or Simla, according to the season. Unlike the officials of the ICS, who served in exile for thirty years, the Viceroy ruled for only four. Unlike them, also, he was appointed directly by the British government. The rituals of social and diplomatic life in the British community revolved around him. Promotion and honours were largely in his gift. As the personal embodiment of British rule, he seemed

to many an immensely powerful figure. But, in practice, his freedom of action was bound by the fact that he could act only through the class of permanent officials, and then only for the short period of his tenure of office. While the Viceroy might favour one policy over another, and his opinion might prove decisive; while he might encourage one official and ignore another, he could scarcely change the whole tendency of British policy, or press for radical changes which conflicted with views widely held by the administrative classes as a whole. This goes far to explain why British concessions to nationalist demands seem so often to have been so hesitant, delayed and half-hearted. Another reason was simply that the Viceroy was answerable to the home government in Britain, which could reverse all his decisions. The Viceroy might have seven hundred servants and a salary twice as big as that of the British Prime Minister, but he was still only a political servant himself, and a temporary one at that.

British rule in India was both oppressive and

11 The hunt, Ootacamund. Note that "Snooty Ooty" nevertheless admitted a number of privileged Indians to its ranks.

enlightened. The officials of the ICS received high salaries and generous pensions, paid out of Indian taxes. The Indian army was used for fighting wars as far away as in China and Abyssinia — also paid for out of Indian taxes. And, despite all the railway-building and irrigation projects, at least 9 million people died of famine in India between 1866 and 1900. As late as 1943 famine was to kill more than a million people in Bengal.

Yet British rule was inspired by high ideals, most powerfully expressed in 1834 by the historian T.B. Macaulay, a liberal, the author of India's legal code, and an ardent advocate of western education for Indians. He foresaw a day, distant perhaps by many centuries, when British rule would be justified by the emergence of an independent but thoroughly anglicized India:

> We are free, we are civilized, to little purpose, if we grudge to any portion of the human race an equal measure of freedom and civilization. Are we to keep the people of India ignorant in order that we may keep them submissive? Or do we think that we can give them knowledge without awakening ambition? Or do we mean to awaken ambition and to provide it with no legitimate vent? . . . To have found a great people sunk in the lowest depths of slavery and superstition, to have so ruled them as to have made them desirous and capable of all the privileges of citizens, would indeed be a title to glory all our own. The sceptre may pass away from us. Unforeseen accidents may derange our most profound schemes of policy. Victory may be inconstant to our arms. But there are triumphs which are followed by no reverse. There is an empire exempt from all natural causes of decay. Those triumphs are the pacific triumphs of reason over barbarism; that empire is the imperishable empire of our arts and morals, our literature, and our laws.

Macaulay's magnificent rhetoric shows the profound contradiction which underlay British rule. Queen Victoria once defined the objectives of empire as being to "protect the poor natives and advance civilization". The problem was that by "advancing civilization", through the building of railways and the introduction of commercial agriculture and western education, one was doing anything but "protecting the poor natives", and at the same time one was ensuring that a class of people would emerge, who would be very disinclined to be treated as "poor natives" at all, protected or otherwise.

Another way of looking at this contradiction is in terms of conflicting ideals of government. On the one hand the British believed in "good government", by which they meant efficient and uncorrupt administration. On the other hand they professed to be leading the administered peoples towards self-government, which meant debate and conflict over public policy. The difficulty lay in how to make the transition from the one to the other.

The British in India believed themselves to be uniquely fitted to rule. They saw themselves as the standard-bearers of a superior culture, honest, well-educated and inspired by the highest ideals of duty and service. Rudyard Kipling, the most famous and in some ways one of the most perceptive of English writers on India, idealized the officials of the ICS who

> kill themselves by overwork, or are worried to death, or broken in health and hope in order that the land may be protected from death and sickness, famine and war, and may eventually become capable of standing alone. It will never stand alone, but the idea is a pretty one, and men are willing to die for it, and yearly the work of pushing and coaxing and scolding the country into good living goes forward.

The British also believed the Indians to be apathetic, quarrelsome and corruptible. They disliked journalists, would-be politicians and western-educated "babus" who could quote the works of liberal philosophers, such as Locke, Bentham and Mill, and who demanded

12 Imperial splendour. The Governor of Bombay with attendants.

equal rights for Indians in impeccably grammatical English. In the words of one of Kipling's characters, a woman doctor:

"what's wrong with this country is not in the least political, but an all-round entanglement of physical, social and moral evils and corruptions . . . "

Kipling's own view was that "they want shovels, not sentiments, in this part of the world".

The British were more willing to concede the right to self-government in theory, than to work toward it in practice. The history of India in the twentieth century is largely the story of how that transition was made.

YOUNG HISTORIAN

A

1 How was it that India came to be ruled by a trading company?

2 Find out about these people and how they were involved in Indian affairs: (a) Job Charnock, (b) Robert Clive, (c) Warren Hastings, (d) Arthur Wellesley (Duke of Wellington), and (e) Lord William Bentinck.

3 What were the strengths and weaknesses of the Viceroy's position?

4 How did the British justify their position as rulers of India?

5 Explain the meaning of (a) Muslims, (b) anarchy, (c) elite, (d) vaccination, (e) census, (f) anglicized.

B

1 Imagine you are a young British official who has just started working in India around 1900. Write a letter to your parents in England telling them about your work and your life in India.

2 Write a dialogue between a British official and an Indian nationalist arguing the case for and against the continuance of British rule in India.

C

Write a series of headlines showing the sort of news of India that might have appeared in the British newspapers around 1900.

D

Draw a diagram showing how the government of India was organized. You should mark in the British Prime Minister, the Secretary of State for India, the Viceroy, the provincial governments, the district officers, the army and the princely states.

POWER-SHARING 1885-1919

THE BIRTH OF NATIONALISM

Modern nationalism, the belief that people with a common history should form a separate, self-governing, independent state, originated in Europe and came to India through western education. British rule was justified by the belief that it spread the values of the world's most highly developed civilization. One way in which these values were spread was through the universities of Bombay, Bengal and Madras, established in 1857. Here young Indian men could read the works of the intellectual giants of Victorian England, Jeremy Bentham, J.S. Mill and T.B. Macaulay, and prepare themselves for employment in government service, commerce or the liberal professions, such as law and journalism. Education introduced to a small Indian elite the novel ideas of individual rights and constitutional government, which were supposed to be the triumphant outcome of England's long history. These ideals did not, of course, apply to the way in which the British ruled India.

If the impact of western ideas was one powerful force in awakening Indian nationalism, the development of communications was certainly another. For many centuries the different parts of the sub-continent had shared a common way of life, based on caste and Hindu beliefs and festivals, but they had been divided by language, distance and varying economic fortunes. The starvation of a Bengali-speaking peasant farmer could mean little to a Gujarati-speaking merchant prospering on the fortunes of a good harvest thousands of miles away. No bonds of feeling could cross the gulf of ignorance and miles which separated them; for all practical purposes, they might as well have lived on separate planets.

Railways and the English language began to change all that, but not overnight and not at a steady and even pace. Undoubtedly, the literate, city-dwelling clerks and merchants began to think of themselves as "Indian", rather than as members of a particular caste or Hindu sect, before the peasants did. And they probably began to think of the peasants as "Indians" before the peasants did as well. Railways and roads made journeys between different parts of India a matter of days and hours rather than months and weeks. English provided a common language in which all educated Indians could grumble about British rule. The opening of the Suez Canal (1869) stimulated the development of cash-crop agriculture in India, by shortening and cheapening the journey from the tea- and jute-plantations to the factories and cities of Europe. The general pace of economic change quickened in consequence. In 1880 there were 22 jute mills in India, by 1914 there were 64. Over the same period the number of cotton mills rose from 58 to 264, despite the fact that these infant industries were unprotected by tariffs against the competition of Lancashire imports. And a major step towards Indian industrialization was taken in 1907, with the foundation of the Tata's Iron and Steel Company.

13 The railway was itself a symbol of British rule and the timetable stood for the order and regularity it strove to represent.

Great Indian Peninsula Railway.

(Incorporated in England).

TIME TABLE.
—:0:—

SPECIAL TRAIN

FOR HIS EXCELLENCY

Baron Chelmsford, G.M.S.I., G.C.M.G., G.M.I.E., G.C.B.E.,

VICEROY AND GOVERNOR-GENERAL OF INDIA,

AND THE RIGHT HONOURABLE

Edwin Samuel Montagu, P.C., M.P.,

SECRETARY OF STATE FOR INDIA,

and SUITE

From Raichur to Bombay (Victoria Terminus) on the 23rd and 24th December 1917.

Distance from Raichur.	Stations.		Standard Time.		Remarks.
MILES.			H.	M.	
	Sunday, 23rd December 1917.				
....	Raichur	Arr.	9	20	From M. & S. M. Railway.
		Dep.	10	0	Breakfast.
74	Shahabad	Arr.	13	15	Lunch.
		Dep.	13	55	
121	Dudhni	Arr.	16	25	Afternoon Tea.
		Dep.	16	35	
160	Sholapur	Arr.	18	28	
		Dep.	18	40	
181	Mohol	Arr.	19	25	Hot Water.
		Dep.	19	39	
191	Angar	Arr.	20	0	Dinner.
		Dep.	21	0	
	Monday, 24th December 1917.				
277	Dhond Junction	Arr.	0	50	
		Dep.	1	5	
324	Poona	Arr.	2	30	
		Dep.	2	55	
389	Neral	Arr.	6	45	Early Tea.
		Dep.	7	0	Hot Water.
410	Kalyan	Arr.	7	33	
		Dep.	7	38	
443	Bombay	Arr.	8	30	

GENERAL TRAFFIC MANAGER'S OFFICE, }
Bombay, the 18th December 1917. }

A. C. RUMBOLL,
General Traffic Manager.

G. I. P. Ry. Press No. 1998 - 40 - 18-12-1917-18.

14 Even *Punch* readers were expected to see that India was the partner of the Raj in its own subjection.

PUNCH, OR THE LONDON CHARIVARI.—June 13, 1896.

AN APPEAL.

INDIA. "I HAVE FOUND THE *MEN*, SAHIB!—WHY SHOULD I FIND THE *MONEY TOO*?"
JOHN BULL. "'PON MY WORD, MY DEAR, I REALLY DON'T SEE WHY YOU SHOULD!"

THE INDIAN NATIONAL CONGRESS

It was against the background of increasing social and economic change that the first meeting of the Indian National Congress was held in Bombay on 28 December 1885. The participants came, significantly, from every province of British India. Equally significant was the fact that more than half were Hindus and only two Muslims, the rest being Parsis or Jains. From its origins, Congress was characterized by a Hindu predominance, which made it difficult for Muslims to accept its claim to represent all Indians, regardless of their religious allegiance.

The founder members of the Congress were, to a man, representative of the new Indian middle class, which had grown out of the opportunities in government service, commerce, and the professions created by British rule. All of them spoke English and more than half of them were lawyers. The others were journalists, teachers and businessmen. Their demands were both political and economic. Politically, they wished to see direct House of Commons control of Indian affairs, the election of non-official representatives to the Supreme and provincial legislature councils, and equality of opportunity in recruitment for the ICS. Their economic grievances revolved around the level of "Home Charges" (i.e. defence spending and pensions to former ICS staff, paid for out of taxes raised in India), which they regarded as an unreasonable burden on the country's resources, and the lack of tariffs on British imported manufactures, which they regarded as a handicap to the growth of India's own industries. It is important to note, however, that the proceedings of the Congress included a specific declaration of loyalty to the British Crown. It did not, therefore, begin its life as an organization dedicated to the cause of Indian independence, but simply as an association seeking reforms within the framework of continued British rule. Certainly, most British opinion felt quite able to ignore the Congress as more irrelevant than irritating. Nevertheless, Congress continued to hold annual meetings, attracting more than 600 in 1887 and more

than twice as many again in the following year.

As the Congress movement grew, its members began to divide in their opinions. One tendency was represented by Gopal Krishna Gokhale (1866-1915), a teacher and social reformer, who was committed to bringing about change through reasoned argument. He believed that the British sense of fairness would eventually lead them to concede that the principles of liberal rule should be applied to Indians as well as to Europeans and that India should eventually be granted self-government within the Empire. A contrary tendency was represented by Bal Gangadhar Tilak (1856-1920), who had taught with Gokhale at Fergusson College, but who, unlike his former colleague, had little faith in British justice. A skilful journalist, Tilak used his newspaper *Kesari* (Lion) and the revived Ganapati and Shivaji festivals to promote pride in Hindu traditions and Marathi culture and history, and to protest against uncritical admiration of everything western. Jailed in 1897 for seditious writings, Tilak won the popular title of "Lokamanya" (revered by the people) for his opposition to British rule, and thus became one of the earliest nationalists to attract the support of the uneducated masses. Tilak asserted that "No one gets anything by begging", and argued that agitation was the only effective strategy to follow.

THE PARTITION OF BENGAL

Curzon, in 1900, saw Congress "tottering to its fall" and hoped to "assist it to a peaceful demise". Instead, he was to see it become stronger than ever. Partly this was due to external events. Japan's victory over Russia in 1905 was an immense stimulus to nationalists all over Asia, proving definitively that Europeans were not invincible in battle. Revolutions in Persia (1906) and Turkey (1908) showed a new spirit stirring across the continent, a demand for freedom from foreign rule and the strength that it was believed would come from the adoption of western technology and systems

15 Curzon, the most viceregal of viceroys — arrogant, conscientious and deeply aware of his responsibilities.

of government. And the example of Sinn Fein in Ireland (1902-22) showed to Indians in particular that British rule could be challenged by force.

But these distant movements, important though they were in provoking dreams and ambitions, were less dramatic in their impact on Indian politics than the actions of the Viceroy himself. In 1905 Curzon, believing that, with a population of some 80 million, Bengal was far too large to be governed efficiently as a single province, ordered it to be divided. This created an eastern province, with a Muslim majority, and a western province, with large numbers of Bihari- and Oriya-speaking Hindus. In neither of the new provinces were Bengali-speaking Hindus, the largest single group in the old,

undivided province, in a majority. They, therefore, interpreted Curzon's action as a deliberate move to "divide and rule" and thus to weaken Hindu Bengali national feeling. This gave the Congress leaders both a cause to patronize and ready-made supporters to organize.

The anti-partition movement relied at first on such traditional liberal methods as petitions and protests in the press. When these failed to produce any impression, they resorted to more original and more radical tactics, notably a boycott of British goods. Public bonfires were made of Lancashire cottons, and protesters proudly clad themselves in "swadeshi", home-made textiles. In due course, the "swadeshi movement" came to involve the deliberate use of other Indian-made products, such as iron utensils, glass and watches. In 1906 the Congress, for the first time, demanded that "the system of government obtaining in the self-governing British colonies" should be extended to India.

This upsurge of Hindu political activity inspired a Muslim reaction, and in the same year the All-Indian Muslim League held its first meeting in Dacca, capital of the Muslim majority province of East Bengal. Anxious to secure Muslim interests in the face of what its leaders saw as the assertion of Hindu power, the League pledged its loyalty to British rule, approved the partition of Bengal, and condemned the boycott of British goods.

By 1906, therefore, there were four major strands of Indian political activity — the moderates within Congress, who wanted self-rule by constitutional means; the extremists within Congress, who wanted independence through agitation; the Muslims outside Congress, who wanted to safeguard their community's rights under British protection; and a small terrorist movement, which favoured assassination and sabotage as direct methods of protest against British rule. The activities of this last group, which later established overseas bases in Germany, Java and the USA, led the authorities to take a number of repressive steps which fell on moderate and extremist alike and thus reinforced the impression that British rule was both high-handed and unsympathetic to Indian ambitions for greater control of their own affairs.

THE MORLEY-MINTO REFORMS

The anti-partition protest movement shook British complacency by revealing an unsuspected gulf between the rulers and the ruled. The British response, known as the Morley-Minto reforms, was an attempt to close this gulf by making the Raj more of a partnership and less of a dictatorship. Minto, Viceroy from 1905 to 1910, was only too aware of the precariousness of British rule, saying "we are here a small British garrison surrounded by millions". Morley, Head of the India Office after the liberal election victory of 1906 in Britain, was led by the conviction that "reforms may not save the Raj but if they don't, nothing else will". Both men were fully aware of Indian aspirations, but they were obliged to work through the medium of the ICS, which solidly opposed concessions to Indian nationalism. They were not willing to revoke the partition of Bengal, nor, when faced with a wave of terrorist bombings and assassinations, did they hesitate to impose restrictions on the liberties of the press and the public. In the face of this firmness, the Indian National Congress split in 1907, but the extremist minority lost ground against the moderates when in 1908 Tilak was tried for sedition and sentenced to six years' imprisonment.

Despite this background of unrest, the Morley-Minto regime pressed ahead with plans to increase Indian participation in government, through the Indian Councils Act (1909). For the first time, an Indian member was to be appointed to the Viceroy's Executive Council, and two Indians were to be added to the Secretary of State's Indian Council in London. Indian representation on the Legislative Council was likewise enlarged, and some of the new members were to be elected. On the provincial legislative councils there were henceforth to be more elected Indian members than nominated official members. Significantly, a proportion of the seats on the Imperial and some provincial legislative councils were specially reserved for Muslims, and Muslim voters were recognized as a separate electorate. Some Indian nationalists, both at the time and later, attacked this arrangement as an infringement of democratic principles (it would give the Muslims more seats than their numbers strictly merited) and a deliberate encouragement to Muslim separation, yet another proof of "divide and rule" tactics to perpetuate British rule. The British saw this special provision for Muslim representation rather differently, as a proper safeguard for the rights of a minority.

It was hoped that these reforms would, as Morley put it in a letter to Minto,

enable the Government the better to realise the wants, interests and sentiments of the

24

governed and, on the other hand, ... give the governed a better chance of understanding, as occasion arises, the case for the Government.

The aim was not to end British rule, but to encourage Indians to accept it and work in partnership with it. Because the legislative councils were now allowed, for the first time, to debate budgets and make amendments to resolutions, it was inevitable that Indian views would be given a greater meaning. But this did not mean that they would be acted upon, and thus Gokhale's repeated demands for the introduction of free elementary education came to nothing. Nor was there any end to the curtailment of civil rights brought about by the government's anti-terrorist campaign. Indian opinion was, however, gratified by the re-unification of Bengal in 1911 and the shifting of the capital from Calcutta to Delhi, once the site of Mughal imperial splendour, in 1912. National pride was further stimulated by the award of the Nobel Prize for Literature to the Bengali poet, Rabindranath Tagore.

16 The Delhi Durbar, 1911 — Indian princes ceremoniously pay homage to the King — Emperor George V.

THE FIRST WORLD WAR

The possibility of gradual political change in India was shattered, however, by the outbreak of war in Europe in the autumn of 1914. Despite the fact that, to the vast majority of Indians, both the origins of the conflict and the principal enemies facing Britain were quite unknown, there was a great outburst of support for the British cause. *The Bengalee*, a Calcutta newspaper, declared that

> we sink our differences and offer all that we possess in defence of the great Empire with

which the future prosperity and advancement of our people are bound up.

Congress itself pledged its "firm resolve to stand by the Empire at all hazards and at all costs", no doubt believing that this loyalty would be rewarded politically in due course. Not only the princes, but even Tilak and Gandhi encouraged Indians to support the war effort.

And India's contribution was to be very great. The Imperial Legislative Council voted a gift of £100 million (a sum equal to an entire year's revenue) and sent £80 million worth of military supplies, 5 million tons of wheat and £137 million worth of jute and sacks. More than one million Indians served as troops and labourers in Europe, the Middle East and East Africa. Thirty-six thousand were killed and more than twice that number wounded.

Indians were at first delighted by the bravery

17 War loan train. India was expected to supply not only men and materials but also cash and credit for the British war effort.

of Indian troops and by Indian membership of the Imperial War Cabinet, which seemed a recognition of India's importance. But as the war dragged on, a current of anti-British feeling began to emerge, fed by several streams of discontent. The death of Gokhale in 1915 removed a moderating influence soon after Tilak's release from prison. Britain's failure to win an early victory weakened her carefully maintained image of military prowess. When General Townshend surrendered to the Turks with 10,000, mostly Indian, troops at Kut in 1916, the image was shaken still further. Local and global issues seemed to combine to weaken Indian acceptance of British rule. Heavy war taxes, inflation and over-recruiting in the Punjab by press-gang methods created

discontent. Muslims resented fighting against the Ottoman Empire, the world's greatest Muslim state. The fall of the Tsarist regime in Russia in 1917 seemed to suggest that no power was too mighty to be overthrown, and US President Woodrow Wilson's declaration of the right of subject peoples to "self-determination" inspired Asian nationalists to ask why this principle should apply only in Europe.

In December 1916 Congress and the Muslim League met simultaneously in Lucknow and called for dominion status for India and a much stronger elected element in government. At the same time the "Lucknow Pact", engineered by Tilak and Mohammed Ali Jinnah, pledged Congress to recognize the Muslims as a separate electorate with the right to more seats in the legislatures than their numbers alone would justify.

18 Indian troops watch an operation under chloroform at a field-dressing station.

To head off demands for Home Rule, the new Secretary of State for India, Edwin Montagu, announced in August 1917 that British policy would henceforth involve

the increasing association of Indians in every branch of the administration and the gradual development of self-governing institutions with a view to the progressive realisation of responsible government in India as an integral part of the British Empire.

He warned, however, that

progress in this policy can only be achieved by successive stages. The British Government and the Government of India . . . must be the judges of the time and measure of each advance, and they must be guided by the co-operation received from those upon whom new opportunities of service will thus be conferred and by the extent to which it is found that confidence can be reposed in their sense of responsibility.

Montagu and Lord Chelmsford, the Viceroy, worked out a new scheme for the government of India, which Congress rejected as "disappointing and unsatisfactory" and which the Muslim League also condemned. Some moderates, however, left Congress and formed the National Liberal Federation (November 1918) to co-operate with the proposed reforms.

THE AMRITSAR MASSACRE

Against the background of a massive influenza epidemic, which killed at least 5 million, discontent continued as the war ended. Demobilized soldiers found themselves once again "natives" rather than British allies, and Indian members of the ICS were disgruntled to see British officials returning from war service to resume the highest posts. In March 1918, to strengthen its hand against possible terrorism, the government passed, against the wishes of every Indian member of the Imperial Legisla-

19 Remediable damage — the National Bank destroyed by Amritsar rioters.

tive Council, the Rowlatt Acts, which allowed the authorities to imprison agitators without trial and judges to try cases without juries. In fact, the powers granted by the Acts were never to be used, but the damage had been done. India's war-time loyalty and sacrifices were apparently to be rewarded by extension into peace-time of emergency controls. Gandhi called for a "hartal", a day without work, to protest against the Acts. On 10 April 1918 the arrest of local nationalist leaders in the Punjab sparked off rioting and arson which led to the deaths of five Englishmen. On 13 April at Amritsar the local commander, General R.E.H. Dyer, ordered his Gurkha troops to open fire on a crowd of 10,000 unarmed protesters. No warning was given. Three hundred and seventy-nine people were killed and more than 1,200 wounded in ten minutes. No medical attention was given to the wounded.

If Indian opinion was horrified at the news of the Amritsar massacre, it was outraged at the British reaction to it. Although Dyer was relieved of his command, the Lieutenant Governor of the Punjab approved his action and so did a majority of the House of Lords. Public subscription in England raised a purse of thousands of pounds and paid for a presentation sword for Dyer, inscribed "Saviour of the Punjab".

Testifying before the Hunter Committee appointed to inquire into the massacre, Dyer defended his action by arguing that

It was no longer a question of merely dispersing the crowd but one of producing a sufficient moral effect, from a military point of view, not only on those who were present, but more specially throughout the Punjab.

In its report, however, the Committee took the view that

he was not entitled to select for punishment an unarmed crowd which, when he inflicted that punishment, had committed no act of violence, had made no attempt to oppose

him by force, and many members of which must have been unaware that they were disobeying his order.

The Times was even more forceful in its condemnation:

> General Dyer's duty . . . was to restore and maintain order in Amritsar . . . which he had already done. It was no part of his duty to attempt to strike terror into the Punjab generally by wholesale massacre.

These belated condemnations came too late to soften Indian anger. Gandhi, having returned to the government the medals he had been awarded in the South African War, denounced British rule as not merely alien but "satanic" and declared:

> I consider the existing system of government to be wholly bad and requiring special

national effort to end or mend it . . . . I can take no pride in calling the Empire mine or in describing myself as a citizen.

THE GOVERNMENT OF INDIA ACT

The atmosphere of hatred and mistrust generated by the Amritsar massacre was scarcely helpful to the experiment in power-sharing, embodied in the Government of India Act (1919), which carried into effect the main proposals of the Montagu-Chelmsford report:

(a) The Viceroy's Legislative Council was to become a parliament, consisting of a Council of State with 60 members (20 appointed, the rest elected by an electorate of 17,000) and an Assembly of 140 members, of whom 100 would be elected by an electorate of one million.

20   India's Parliament, built as part of Lutyens' show piece capital "New Delhi".

(b)   Provincial legislative councils were to be 70 per cent elected by an electorate of 5 million.

(c)   Voting rights would be based on property and educational qualifications.

(d)   Under the principle of "dyarchy", the various tasks of government in the provinces would be shared between British and Indian ministers. Police matters, justice and land revenue were "reserved" to British control, but the "nation-building" departments such as education, health and public works were "transferred" into Indian hands.

The first parliament elected under the new system met in Delhi in February 1921, while members of the National Liberal Federation began to carry out reforms in Bengal, Bombay and the United Provinces. Unionist and Justice Party governments in Punjab and Madras respectively showed that regionally based political parties might also develop strongly, given time. But these first steps towards "responsible government" were overshadowed by the organization of a massive campaign of "non-cooperation", which was to transform the nationalist cause into a true mass movement.

YOUNG HISTORIAN

A

1 Explain why (a) western education, (b) railways, and (c) external political events were particularly important in the emergence of an Indian nationalist movement.

2 Summarize the earliest demands of the Congress movement and explain how and when these demands changed.

3 Write a dialogue between Gokhale and Tilak in which they explain their differing attitudes towards British rule.

4 Outline the ways in which Hindus and Muslims were divided in this period.

5 Do you think British policy towards India in this period is better described as one of "divide and rule" or of "partnership"?

6 Explain the meaning of (a) cash-crop, (b) tariff, (c) partition, (d) swadeshi, (e) sedition.

B

Write an account of:
(a) the first meeting of the Indian National Congress, OR
(b) the struggle over the partition of Bengal, OR
(c) the Amritsar massacre
from the viewpoint of (a) an Indian nationalist, and (b) a British official.

C

Write a series of headlines for an Indian nationalist newspaper, covering the major events of the years 1909-1919.

D

Design a poster (a) against British rule in India, or (b) to recruit Indians to fight for Britain in the First World War.

SWARAJ 1919–1935

GANDHI'S NON-COOPERATION CAMPAIGN

In August 1920 Tilak died, leaving Gandhi as the most important Congress leader. Gandhi proposed a comprehensive programme of non-cooperation, involving a general boycott of British goods, schools, courts, councils and elections. Congress gave its approval and also committed itself to "the attainment of swaraj [self-government] by peaceful and legitimate means". Gandhi's campaign of non-cooperation was also supported by many Muslims, who were angered by the Treaty of Sèvres which threatened to carve up the defeated Ottoman Empire. Hindus and Muslims proclaimed their united opposition to British rule.

Events soon showed that, while Gandhi had the authority to start a campaign of non-cooperation, he did not have the power to control it. Although schools were disrupted, and only one third of the electorate turned out to vote for the provincial legislative councils, few Indians resigned from official service, and, despite Gandhi's efforts, the movement soon lost its non-violent character, because the protesters lacked both unity and discipline. Peasants took advantage of the situation to riot against local landlords and moneylenders. In Malabar the Moplahs, a Muslim sect descended from Arab traders, attacked local Hindus,

21 Followers of Gandhi, clad in home-made cloth, surround a symbolic spinning-wheel (1922).

killing hundreds. In February 1922 a mob burned to death twenty-two policemen in their station at Chauri Chaura in the United Provinces. Appalled, Gandhi called off the campaign and was soon after arrested and sentenced to six years' imprisonment. "The foetid smell of violence is still powerful," he wrote to Nehru. "The movement has consciously drifted from the right path."

The non-cooperation campaign of 1920-22 did not overthrow British rule, but it did shake it. It did not "stop the machine" of the administration, but it did put it under great strain. The government had lost its old self-confidence and the nationalists, for all their disagreements and confusions over aims and methods, had a new sense of their power. Congress was no longer a middle-class association, but a mass movement with deeper roots and stronger, more confident leaders.

MODERATE PROGRESS

For the moment, however, the initiative lay with the moderates, and in 1923 C.R. Das

persuaded Congress to sponsor the Swaraj party to contest elections. The original plan was to gain office and then obstruct the working of the government from within, just as the Irish Nationalists had done in Britain half a century before. But once in power, some Congress politicians could not resist the temptation to exercise their new authority and soon found themselves cooperating with the government.

As political tensions eased, constructive reform became possible. The Rowlatt Acts were abolished and so was the excise on cotton. India gained complete control of her tariffs and achieved full membership of the League of Nations. An increasing proportion of the Indian army officer corps was drawn from the Indian population, and the Lee Commission looked forward to an equal balance between British and Indian officials in the ICS. To many, however, progress was deplorably slow. As Gandhi himself pointed out, at the end of the decade the government was still spending more on police and prisons than on education, more on pensions than on public health.

GANDHI'S CAMPAIGN OF CIVIL DISOBEDIENCE

In 1927 the British government appointed the Simon Commission to examine the working of the Montagu-Chelmsford system and to make recommendations for further reform. The seven members of the Commission did not, however, include a single Indian, and enraged nationalists denounced it as "a deliberate insult to the people of India". Congress boycotted its sessions

22 Bombay demonstrators cheerfully reject the enquiries of the Simon Commission (1928).

and organized demonstrations wherever its members went. The general impression of popular unrest thus created was strengthened by a series of major strikes in the textile mills of Bombay and on the railways.

In 1928 the major Indian parties met together at Lucknow, and the majority approved a report, drawn up by the veteran moderate Motilal Nehru, which called for dominion status, full self-government and the abolition of separate communal electorates (Jinnah and many other Muslims did not accept this last provision). Younger, more radical members, such as Jawaharlal Nehru and Subhas Chandra Bose, wanted to go further and called for complete independence outside the British Empire. At this point, Gandhi re-entered active politics to promote a compromise, which would head off the possibility of a split between the moderates and the extremists; it was, therefore, agreed that unless dominion status had been achieved by the end of 1929, the goal would become complete independence and another

23 Salt-boilers defy the law. Note the spinning-wheel on the flag.

campaign of civil disobedience would be launched.

In October 1929, without waiting for the report of the Simon Commission, the Viceroy, Lord Irwin, announced that the British would grant dominion status at some future time and that a Round Table conference would be called to work out the next steps forward. This was too vague for the more radical Congress leaders and, rather than see the movement split and possibly drift towards violence, Gandhi went ahead with his campaign of civil disobedience.

Rather than institute a general boycott, as in 1920-22, Gandhi chose this time to focus his protest on the salt-tax, which everyone, rich or poor, had to pay. Making salt without paying the tax was illegal. Gandhi informed the authorities that he was going to break the law and on 12 March 1930 set out to march through Gujarat to the coast. At first, the government tried to ignore the campaign, but thousands flocked to hear and follow Gandhi in his protest. On 6 April, on the sea-shore at Dandi, before crowds of onlookers and journalists, Gandhi ceremoniously broke the law by picking up a lump of natural salt. This simple, non-violent gesture of defiance compelled the admiration of millions of Indians and, indeed, of many British people. The protest movement spread rapidly. In some places there were outbreaks of violence. On 18 April eight guards were killed when the armoury at Chittagong was raided, and on 24 April there was a major riot in Peshawar. But, even after Gandhi's arrest on 4 May, the non-violence campaign lost none of its momentum. On 21 May protesters marched on the salt-works at Dharasave, 150 miles north of Bombay. Armed only with ropes to pull down barbed-wire fences and barriers, the 2,500-strong crowd suffered 300 casualties and 2 deaths. An American newspaper correspondent described their silent, disciplined assault:

> They marched steadily, with heads up, without the encouragement of music or cheering . . . . There was no fight, no struggle, the marchers simply walked forward until struck down. There were no outcries, only groans after they fell.

By the end of the year some one hundred thousand people had been arrested and one hundred killed by the police, and scores of newspapers had been closed down. A notable feature of the campaign was the emergence of women as marchers and speakers. Another was the fact that the Muslims did not, on the whole, take part.

THE ROUND TABLE CONFERENCES

In November 1930 a Round Table conference at last met in London, but without any representatives from Congress, although the Liberals, the Muslim League and sixteen princes took part. Even without Congress participation, the conference was not entirely useless because, rather surprisingly, the princes agreed to join a future Indian federation. Nevertheless, it was obvious that further progress could not be made without the participation of Congress. In January 1931 Gandhi was released from prison and began a series of discussions with Lord Irwin which resulted in an agreement whereby Gandhi would call off the civil disobedience campaign and take part in the next Round Table conference, while Irwin would order the release of all jailed protesters who had not been guilty of violence. (It was also agreed that the Salt Acts would not be repealed but that peasants would be allowed to make salt for their own use though not for sale.)

The second Round Table conference opened in September 1931, with Gandhi as the sole representative of the entire Congress movement. No agreement was reached, however, on the question of separate representation for Muslims, untouchables and other minorities. The British wanted constitutional safeguards for them. Gandhi insisted that Congress was not a Hindu interest-group but that it represented all Indians, regardless of their belief. The conference ended in stalemate and Gandhi renewed his campaign of non-cooperation.

The new Viceroy, Lord Willingdon, backed by the new Conservative-dominated "National Government" in Britain, was determined to crush the protest movement. Gandhi was soon arrested, along with other Congress leaders. Congress itself was outlawed and public meetings were banned.

Even in prison, however, Gandhi continued to exercise a decisive influence on events. Because the second Round Table conference had failed to settle the issue of minority representation, the British in August 1932 announced a "Communal Award", confirming the system of separate electorates and constituencies for minorities such as the Muslims, Sikhs and Christians, and, significantly, for the first time extending it to India's 50 million "scheduled castes" (untouchables). Gandhi, fearing the emergence of another divisive force which would further split the solidarity of the nationalist movement, denounced separate provision for the untouchables and threatened to fast to death. When his life was almost despaired of, the untouchable leader, B.R. Ambedkar, agreed to renounce his former acceptance of the Communal Award. In return, Gandhi agreed that the untouchables should have a larger number of representatives, chosen by themselves in a primary election, but elected by the general Hindu electorate, in which they would be included.

THE GOVERNMENT OF INDIA ACT 1935

The British, meanwhile, having held a third Round Table conference to little effect (November-December 1932), began to prepare a new constitution for India, based on the report of the Simon Commission and the results of the Round Table conferences. This was embodied in the Government of India Act of 1935, the longest statute ever passed by a British Parliament. The main provisions of the Act were that:

(a) "Responsible government" was to be established in the provinces with ministers responsible to an electorate of 40 million. Governors retained emergency powers of intervention but were expected to use them only in the most exceptional circumstances (e.g. to protect minorities).

Self-government was thus substantially established at the provincial level.

(b) "Dyarchy" was to be established at the central government level. The new legislature would consist of a Council of State and an Assembly, in each of which the elected members would out-number the appointed ones, and in each of which a generous proportion of the seats would be set aside for the nominated representatives of the princes. Certain areas of policy (e.g. defence and foreign affairs, the protection of minorities) were still reserved for the Viceroy, however; the new constitution did not, therefore, represent full dominion status such as was enjoyed by Australia or Canada.

Large sections of the Act, notably those dealing with the question of relations between the central government and the provinces, were later to be incorporated in the constitution of independent India. But at the time it was denounced by Nehru as "a charter of slavery" and by Bose as intended "not for self-government but for maintaining British rule". Because the princely states were not, in fact, persuaded to join the new federation, the federal provisions of the Act never came into force. But the brief experience of provincial self-government which preceded the outbreak of the Second World War was sufficient to demonstrate not only the abilities of the nationalist leaders but also their divisions, with the most profound of consequences.

24 (Overleaf)   The Round Table Conference. The table was not quite round and the conference, in the absence of several key Indian leaders, not quite a conference.

INDIAN
ROUND-TABLE CONFERENCE
1930-31

Kelen
1931

YOUNG HISTORIAN

A

1. Explain why the Indian nationalist movement turned to the tactics of non-cooperation during this period. What were the main results of this policy?
2. Why were Gandhi and the other Congress leaders so opposed to separate political status for Muslims, untouchables and other such groups?
3. Summarize the progress which was made by Indians during this period in gaining greater control of their own affairs.
4. Explain the meaning of: (a) swaraj, (b) boycott, (c) dominion status, (d) dyarchy.

B

Imagine you are a young Indian nationalist following Gandhi's salt march. Write a letter to your parents explaining why you have joined it and describing the events that happen as a result.

C

Write a series of headlines covering the main events between 1923 and 1935.

D

Draw a map which shows where the main political events of this period took place.

PARTIES AND PARTITION 1935-1947

In February 1937 elections were held for the new provincial legislative councils. Congress put up candidates with a view to obstructing the system from within and forcing the British to agree to the calling of a constituent assembly to draw up an independence constitution. When the results were declared, Congress was once again seen to be the strongest single political group in India, winning outright control of six provinces and having effective control of two more. Faced with the possibility of exercising power, Congress politicians chose to do so. Congress ministries were eventually formed, leading to the release of political prisoners, the restoration of civil liberties and a number of social and agricultural reforms. More important, however, was the refusal of the Congress leadership to create coalition cabinets in partnership with the Muslim League.

Jinnah, having taken over the Muslim League in 1935, campaigned vigorously in provinces with large Muslim minorities and looked forward to governing these in coalition with the Congress. Congress, however, although it appointed its own Muslim members to office, refused to appoint League Muslims. Jinnah had to choose between letting Congress take over the League and trying to find another way for the League to gain power. He chose the latter course.

PAKISTAN

In 1930 the poet, Sir Muhammad Iqbal, the president of the Muslim League for that year, had suggested that the Muslim-minority regions of the northwest should have complete control of their internal affairs within a loose Indian Federation. In 1933 Chaudhuri Rahmat Ali in Cambridge coined the word "Pakistan" to describe this area, meaning in Urdu "Land of the Pure", and made from the initial letters of the Muslim-dominated regions of the *P*unjab, the *A*fghan frontier, *K*ashmir and *S*ind plus the Persian "stan", meaning "country". Pakistan as a separate Muslim state had begun to be defined, at least in location. By refusing partnership with Jinnah in 1937, Congress set him on the path to separation. Pakistan was to be no longer a dream but an objective. During 1938 Gandhi and Jinnah tried to reach an understanding, but Congress refused to recongnize the League's claim to be the sole spokesman for India's Muslims and negotiations between the two parties broke down completely.

THE SECOND WORLD WAR

When war broke out in Europe in 1939, the Viceroy declared India to be at war, alongside Britain, without consulting any of the nationalist leaders. All the Congress provincial ministries resigned in protest. Jinnah organized a Muslim "Day of Thanksgiving", to celebrate the Congress withdrawal from power. Over the next few years, with Congress on the side-lines, the League became, in fact, what it had long claimed to be in theory, the representative of the overwhelming majority of Muslims. In March 1940 it called officially for the establishment of

41

separate Muslim states, one consisting of Bengal and Assam in the east, and the other comprising Punjab, Sind, Baluchistan and the North West Frontier Province in the west.

In August 1940 the Viceroy offered the nationalist leaders dominion status "as soon after the war as possible". Both Congress and the League rejected this offer and in October Gandhi launched an individual civil disobedience movement. By May 1941 14,000 of his followers had been arrested.

Japan's rapid conquest of Southeast Asia led the British to make further moves to secure the loyalty of India, and in March 1942 Sir Stafford Cripps arrived with plans for full independence after the war. The provincial legislatures would elect a constituent assembly and India would be free to leave the Commonwealth if she chose to do so. In the meantime, party leaders were invited to join the Viceroy's council, which would, as far as possible, be treated as a fully responsible cabinet. Congress insisted that the new council be granted the full powers of a dominion cabinet, without reservation. Deadlock followed and the Cripps mission ended in failure.

Japan, holding almost all of Burma, now appeared poised to conquer India itself. Gandhi declared that India was endangered only by the British presence and that, left to defend itself, it could defeat the Japanese by a campaign of passive resistance. In August 1942 he called upon the British, therefore, to "Quit India" at once, and began another campaign of civil disobedience. The British immediately arrested the Congress leadership and, when communications were deliberately disrupted in Bihar and the United Provinces, put down the movement by force. About one thousand lives were lost in the disturbances and 60,000 people arrested.

With the Congress leadership locked up, and the Muslim League and Communist party concentrating on building up their grass-roots support, the initiative now passed to Subhas Chandra Bose. Having been out-manoeuvred by Gandhi in his attempts to take over the leadership of Congress, Bose had fled to Germany in 1941 and then turned up in Japanese-occupied Singapore to recruit an "Indian National Army" from prisoners-of-war and deserters. He pledged

himself to liberate India from British rule, perhaps taking over as a sort of strong-man soldier-statesman. In the event, his "National Army" scarcely affected the fighting and in 1945 Bose died in a plane crash in Taiwan. However, after the war the officers of his army were tried by the British as traitors.

By 1944 the Japanese threat had receded and the Allies had become confident of eventual victory. In India the British authorities turned their attention once more to the problems of post-war settlement and in June 1945 the Viceroy, Field Marshall Wavell, arranged a meeting of nationalist leaders at Simla, aiming to form a new Executive Council which would last until the end of the war against Japan and then arrange for the promised constituent assembly. Congress, however, refused to recognize the League's claim to speak on behalf of all Muslims and, therefore, no agreement was possible regarding the nomination of members for the new Executive Council.

At this time it was still thought that the end of the war was at least a year away, but two unexpected developments changed the whole time-table for constitutional change. In July 1945 a Labour government, pledged to give India independence, was returned to power in Britain. Its leader, Clement Attlee, had been a member of the ill-fated Simon Commission almost twenty years before. In August the dropping of the atomic bombs on Hiroshima and Nagasaki and the ending of Russian neutrality towards Japan brought the war to a sudden close.

THE TRANSFER OF POWER

New elections were then held, at both the central and the local level. The results clarified the struggle for power. At central government level the League won all the seats reserved for Muslims, and the Congress won all but five of the rest. In the provinces the League won 439 of

Nehru

Fucker

M. A. Jinnah

the 494 Muslim seats and Congress won outright majorities in eight provinces. Any future division of power in India would therefore have to satisfy the claims of these two great parties. The British, their army rapidly demobilized with the ending of the war, were in no position to enforce a settlement. Their concern was to withdraw in as orderly a way as possible, and this rested on trying to arrange some sort of compromise between the apparently irreconcilable claims of Congress and the League.

In April 1946 a "Cabinet Mission" arrived in Delhi, with the aim of trying to find a formula which would enable the British to hand over power to a single government of an undivided India. In May, after fruitless discussions with League and Congress leaders the mission put forward its own ingenious plan for a three-tier federation. The central government would control defence, foreign policy and communications, and the provinces would be free to form

intermediate regional groupings to which they could hand over such other powers as they chose. This would enable Muslim areas to control their own affairs to a very great extent but still preserve the over-all unity of India. In June the Cabinet Mission announced the composition of the interim government which was to function until the constitution for India was framed and power transferred into Indian hands. Congress and the Muslim League both interpreted the Cabinet Mission plan differently and, therefore, no agreement was reached between them.

In July 1946 elections for a constituent assembly were held, Congress winning 205 seats and the League 73. However, in this same month, Jinnah called for a day of "Direct Action" to be held on 16 August. Against the general background of food shortages and demobilization, there had already been several outbreaks of violence between Muslims and Hindus. Jinnah's Direct Action day led to a

26 A conference at the Viceroy's House, New Delhi. Mountbatten sits between Nehru (in white cap) and Jinnah (in white jacket).

massive riot in Calcutta, ending with some 4,000 deaths. Other outbreaks then occurred in Bihar, East Bengal and the United Provinces. In December, however, the League still boycotted the first meeting of the constituent assembly which would debate the future of India.

To break the deadlock, the British government announced in February 1947 its "definite intention" to hand over power "into responsible Indian hands" by a date not later than June 1948. Viscount Mountbatten was appointed Viceroy to oversee the difficult transition. At first he hoped to preserve Indian unity, but he soon realized that this was impossible. The

Punjab had become almost ungovernable, as Muslims, Sikhs and Hindus massacred each other, the riots originating in fear and then being sustained by the momentum of vengeance and counter-vengeance. Jinnah remained obstinate in his demand for partition: "I do not care how little you give me, so long as you give it to me completely." Gandhi put forward the only really radical solution — to hand over control of a united India to the Muslim League, rather than to see India divided. When this suggestion was rejected by Congress, he withdrew from further involvement in the search for a political settlement and concentrated on trying to end the violence in the most riot-torn areas of Bengal.

On 3 June 1947 the British announced their plan to establish two successor states to their rule — India and Pakistan. This plan was accepted by both the League and Congress and the date of independence was set for 14 August. Provinces

27 Agony of partition — a stone-throwing riot in Calcutta, 1947.

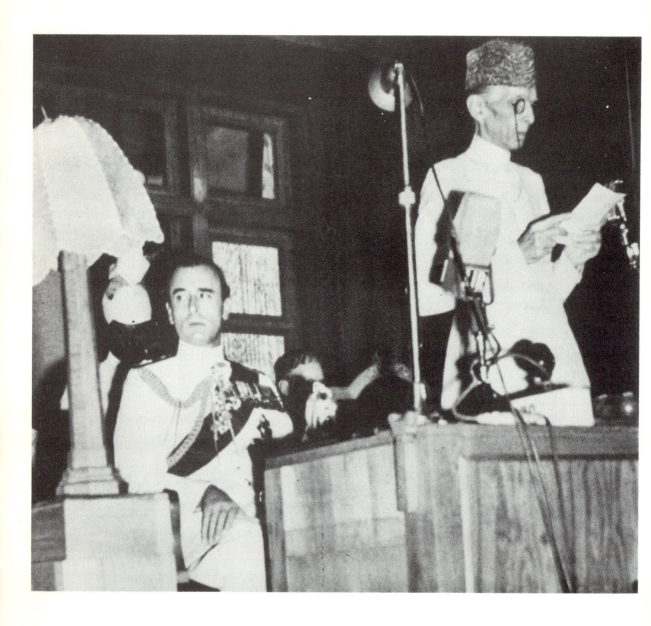

were to opt for India or Pakistan by vote of their legislatures, except for the North West Frontier Province, where the narrow majority of the government made it advisable to hold a referendum. In the Punjab and Bengal the non-Muslim members of the legislatures were given the option of demanding the partition of those provinces and joining the constituent assembly of their choice. This meant, of course, that the non-Muslim parts of the Punjab and Bengal could join the Indian union. By July 1947 the provinces had made their choice. Sind, Baluchistan, North West Frontier Province, West Punjab

28 An apprehensive-looking Mountbatten hears Jinnah's inaugural speech as the first Governor-General of Pakistan.

and East Bengal opted for Pakistan; the rest of the provinces remained with India.

The government of independent India took power on 15 August 1947, with Mountbatten as the first governor-general of the new dominion. The dignity of the ceremonies in Delhi and the general rejoicing of the population could not, however, disguise or moderate the horrendous violence which accompanied the partitions of

Bengal and the Punjab. By September the arrival of refugees bearing tales of horror led to outbreaks of violence in the capital itself. It is estimated that more than 5 million people travelled each way across the new border that cut through the Punjab; and almost half a million Hindus fled from Sind; while more than one million moved from East Pakistan to West Bengal. The exact number who died in the accompanying massacres is not known. Estimates vary from 300,000 to more than one million.

YOUNG HISTORIAN

A
1 Why did Muslims come to demand a separate state for themselves during this period?
2 Contrast the effect of the First and Second World Wars on the Indian Nationalist movement.
3 Why were officers of the Indian National Army tried as traitors after the war? Do you think they were traitors?
4 Why did independence lead to the partition of India?
5 Explain the meaning of (a) constituent assembly, (b) civil liberties, (c) referendum.

B
Imagine you are a refugee from the Punjab. Write a letter to a friend in Delhi, explaining why you are leaving your home and asking him to help you.

C
Write a series of headlines covering the main events between 1942 and 1947.

D
Design a poster for the "Quit India" movement.

NATION-MAKERS: GANDHI AND NEHRU

GANDHI

Mohandas Karamchand Gandhi was born in 1869, the son of the chief minister of a small princely state in Gujarat. Politics were, therefore, part of his background from the very beginning; but, thanks largely to the influence of his pious mother, his early years were dominated by religion. The beliefs and principles basic to his family's way of life included: ahimsā (non-violence towards all living things); vegetarianism; fasting for self-discipline; and tolerance of the beliefs of others.

Gandhi's school record was not a good one, but in 1887 he managed to enter college and in the following year his family sent him to England to study law. The move from rural India to teeming London presented him with many challenges. His struggle to keep to his vegetarian diet led him to meet English vegetarians, many of them socialists and intellectuals, such as George Bernard Shaw. Gandhi had come to England believing it to be "a land of philosophers and poets, the very centre of civilization". Many of his new friends, however, were extremely critical of social conditions in England and especially of its worship of wealth, to the damage of men and communities.

When he returned to India in 1891, Gandhi found that he did not have a sufficiently forceful personality to enable him to make a success of the law. He, therefore, accepted employment with an Indian trading firm in South Africa. Here he experienced many of the painful and humiliating acts of discrimination which were commonly practised by the white population against the thousands of Indians who had migrated there in their search for work. Thrown out of a first-class railway carriage, beaten up for refusing to give up stage-coach seats for a white passenger, barred from hotels reserved "for Europeans only", Gandhi became determined to stand up for his rights and those of his countrymen. In 1894 he organized the Indian community in Natal to oppose a bill which would deprive them of the vote. The bill was passed, but the Indians for the first time made their voice heard, not only in Natal but in India and England as well. More important still, Gandhi had, for the first time, overcome his personal shyness and taken a leading part in a political campaign.

In 1896 Gandhi returned to India to arouse support for the plight of Indians overseas. When he went back again to Durban, Natal, a white mob almost lynched him, but he refused to prosecute them, although the Colonial Secretary, Joseph Chamberlain, had pressed the Natal government to see that the guilty men were punished.

When the Boer War broke out in 1899, Gandhi said that, because Indians claimed the full rights of citizenship in Natal, even though these were denied to them, they were also bound to defend it. He, therefore, raised an 1,100-strong volunteer ambulance corps to tend the wounded. But this gesture did little

29 The young Gandhi, the Europeanized would-be lawyer.

48

Truth is One

Subscription { Single copy As. 2 / One year Rs. 5 / Six months Rs. 3 } Foreign Rs. 7, Sh. 12, $ 3

Young India

A Weekly Journal   **Edited by M. K. Gandhi**

Vol. IX   Ahmedabad: Thursday, April 21, 1927   No. 16

The Story of
My Experiments with Truth
(By M. K. Gandhi)
PART III—CHAPTER XX

In Benares

The journey was from Calcutta to Rajkot, and I wanted to halt at Benares, Agra, Jaypur and Palanpur *en route*. I had not the time to see any more places than these. I stayed a day at each one of these places, and in *dharmashalas* or with Pandas like the ordinary pilgrims, excepting at Palanpur. So far as I can remember I did not spend more than Rs. 31 (including the train fare) on this journey.

In travelling third class I mostly preferred the ordinary to the mail trains, as I knew that the latter used to be crowded, and there was of course the objection of the fare being higher for third class by mail.

The third class compartments were as dirty and the closet arrangements were as bad as today, though there might be a little improvement now. But the difference between the facilities provided for the first and the third classes is out of all proportion to that between the fares for the two classes. Third class passengers are treated like sheep and their comforts are sheep's comforts. In Europe I travelled third—and only once first, just to see what it was like—but there I noticed no such difference between the first and the third classes. In South Africa third class passengers are mostly negroes, yet the third class comforts are better than here. In parts of South Africa third class compartments are provided with sleeping accommodation, and cushioned seats. The accommodation is also regulated, so as to prevent overcrowding, whereas here I have found the regulation limit mostly exceeded.

The indifference of the railway authorities to the comforts of the third class passengers, combined with the dirty and inconsiderate habits of the passengers themselves, makes third class travelling a trial for a passenger with cleanly habits. These uncleanly habits commonly include spitting and throwing of rubbish in the compartment, smoking at all hours and in all places, betel and tobacco chewing and converting the whole carriage into a spittoon, shouting and yelling, and using foul language, regardless the convenience or comfort of fellow passengers. I have noticed little difference between my experience of the third class travelling in 1902 and that of my unbroken third class tours from 1915 to 1919. I can think of only one remedy for this awful state of things, and it is this that educated men should make a point of travelling third class and reforming the habits of the people, as also of never letting the railway authorities rest in peace by complaints wherever necessary, never resorting to bribes or any unlawful means for the sake of their own comforts, and never putting up with infringements of rules on the part of any one concerned.

This, I am sure, will bring about considerable improvement. My serious illness in 1918–19 has unfortunately compelled me practically to give up third class travelling, and it has always been a matter for pain and shame to me, especially because the disability should have come at a time when the agitation for the removal of the hardships of third class passengers was making fair headway. The hardships of poor railway and steamship passengers, accentuated by their bad habits, the undue facilities allowed by Government to foreign trade, and such other things, make an important subject by itself worthy to be taken up by one or two enterprising and persevering workers devoting their full time to it.

But I shall leave the third class passengers at that, and come to my experiences in Benares. I reached there in the morning. I had decided to put up with a *Panda*. Numerous Brahmans surrounded me, as soon as I got out of the train, and I selected the house of one of them who struck me to be comparatively cleaner and better than the rest. It proved to be a good choice. There was a cow in the courtyard of the house which had a storey where I was given my lodging. I did not want to have any food without ablution in the Ganges in the proper orthodox manner. The *Panda* made preparations for it. I had told him beforehand that on no account could I give him more than a rupee and four annas as *dakshina*, and that he should therefore have that in view in making the preparations.

The *Panda* readily assented. ' Be the pilgrim rich or poor,' said he, ' the service is the same in every case. But the amount of *dakshina* we receive depends upon the will and the ability of the pilgrim.' I did not find that the *Panda* at all abridged the usual formalities in my case. The *Puja* was over at twelve o'clock, and I went to the Kashi Vishvanath temple for *darshan*. I was deeply pained by what I saw there. When practising as a barrister in Bombay in 1891, I had occasion to attend a lecture on ' Pilgrimage to Kashi' in the Prarthana Samaj hall. I was therefore prepared for some measure of disappoint-

to change the feelings of the local white population towards the Indians and from 1906 until 1913 Gandhi led a long struggle to uphold the civil rights of the Indian population. It was during this period that he developed the technique of "satyagraha" ("firmness to truth"), a method of non-violent resistance to authority, in which the protester accepted beatings and imprisonment at the hands of the authorities. In the end, Gandhi won a number of important concessions for the Indian community, although discrimination has, of course, continued to the present day.

By the time Gandhi left South Africa, the main principles of his philosophy had been worked out. His life was essentially concerned with a religious quest rather than with a political struggle. In 1936 when he had withdrawn from active politics to live in a small village in central India, Gandhi told a curious and admiring visitor:

I am here to serve no one but myself . . . . Man's ultimate aim is the realisation of God, and all his activities, political, social and religious, have to be guided by the ultimate aim of the vision of God . . . . I am a part and parcel of the whole and I cannot find Him apart from the rest of humanity. My countrymen are my nearest neighbours. They have become so helpless, resourceless and inert that I must concentrate on serving them. If I could persuade myself that I should find Him in a Himalayan cave, I would proceed there immediately. But I know that I cannot find Him apart from humanity.

Gandhi drew on many sources for his ideas. The first major influence was the Sermon on the Mount; the greatest was the Bhagavad-Gita, an ancient work of Hindu philosophy which he first read in an English translation. He also read the Qur'an and Tolstoy and was especially impressed by "Unto This Last", a lengthy criticism of industrial society by the Victorian art critic and writer, John Ruskin. Gandhi agreed wholeheartedly with Ruskin

30 The mature Gandhi — an extract from his autobiography (*Experiments with Truth*) reprinted in his own weekly journal.

that the so-called triumphs of industrial civilization were illusory — "Men can neither drink steam, nor eat stone" — and that the material abundance created by modern technology was more likely to stimulate greed than to satisfy need. In Gandhi's view, "Western nations are groaning under the monster-god of materialism. Their moral growth has become stunted." Inspired by Ruskin's views, he established two communities in South Africa, dedicated to living a simple life of work and study: one at Phoenix, near Durban, and another, Tolstoy Farm, near Johannesburg. On his return to India he was to establish similar settlements at Sābarmati, near Ahmedabad, and at Sevagram, near Wardha. These were intended to provide practical examples of his philosophy in action, for Gandhi believed that it was above all in the villages that the struggle for India's future would be won or lost.

Gandhi certainly possessed great political genius. Skilled in negotiation, he sought compromise wherever possible. As a practising lawyer, he had always regarded it as more important to bring disputants to a reasonable settlement out of court, than to win great victories before judge and jury. His dedication to the art of reconciliation enabled him to hold together a Congress that was all too often divided by personal rivalries and the antagonisms which existed between moderates and extremists. It also enabled him on numerous occasions to intervene courageously and effectively to put a stop to Hindu-Muslim violence.

The basis of Gandhi's political influence in Congress was not, however, his skill in negotiation or diplomacy, but his ability to reach out and move the masses, the millions of illiterate peasants who looked upon him as a "sadhū" or "holy man". Gandhi, in Nehru's words, "nationalized nationalism". When Gandhi returned from South Africa, the poet, Rabindranath Tagore, named him "Mahatma" ("Great Soul"). Soon this was the name by which he was known to millions.

Gandhi was not innocent, but he strove to be pure. He was not blind to the evil in men, British or Indian, Hindu or Muslim, but he tried always to appeal to whatever in them was rational and good. When he could not appeal,

31 "Great Soul" — Gandhi, seven hours after ending a fast in protest against the Calcutta riots of 1947, sets to work on an article for *The Harijan.*

he would try to shame. In September 1947 his fasting stopped the rioting in Calcutta, and in January 1948 he likewise shamed Delhi into a truce. In the long run, it was his appeal to conscience which weakened the resolution of the British to hold on to India at all costs. His non-violent demonstrations showed up the gap between the liberal principles of free speech and fair play by which the British claimed to live and the use of force by which, in the last resort, their rule in India was upheld. As Gandhi told a close British friend:

An Englishman . . . is afraid of nothing physical; but he is very mortally afraid of

his own conscience if . . . you appeal to it, and show him to be in the wrong. He does not like to be rebuked for wrong-doing at first; but he will think it over, and it will get hold of him and hurt him till he does something to put it right.

Gandhi could reach the masses because he tried to live as they did. Unlike many of the nationalist leaders, he was not a Brahmin. In middle age he abandoned western dress and adopted the peasants' dhoti as his costume. He kept strictly to a plain diet, neither smoked nor drank, and used his earnings to support others or the causes for which he struggled. Although he devoted much time to writing newspaper articles, pamphlets and books (his collected works fill more than 80 volumes), he realized that it is not only illiterate people who are moved by the force of example. His fasting became a symbol of his willingness to sacrifice and his determination to succeed. His devotion to the spinning of khadi (home-made yarn) symbolized his belief in living simply, in the dignity of manual labour and in the desirability of self-reliance.

Gandhi wanted to reach the masses for two reasons: to get the British out of India, and to improve their condition. Only a mass movement could both make it impossible for the British to rule effectively and prove to them, at the same time, that their government was not acceptable to the people for whose benefit they claimed it existed. But the removal of the British was not an end in itself but a preliminary to the re-birth of India, a re-birth which the

32 The spinner — Gandhi believed in the force of example as much as of persuasion.

non-violent struggle for independence would itself assist. Gandhi asserted that:

If India has patience enough to go through the fire of suffering and to resist any unlawful encroachment upon its own civilization which, imperfect though it undoubtedly is, has hitherto stood the ravages of time, she can make a lasting contribution to the peace and solid progress of the world.

Gandhi believed that traditional Hindu civilization, based on such ideals as respect for life and the absence of competition, upheld values which could guide the life of all mankind. But this is not to say that Gandhi accepted the Hindu heritage uncritically. He was, in particular, determined to raise the status of women and to bring the untouchables, whom he re-named "harijans" ("Children of God"),

into the community. This brought him into conflict with Brahmins, who regarded themselves as the guardians of orthodoxy and opposed his attempts to encourage harijans to use the same wells and temples as other people.

What Gandhi looked for was a spiritual and moral improvement in the Indian nation's life. He wanted to make men not richer but better. He viewed political power and economic growth with suspicion. While not opposed to modern technology as such, he thought its rapid introduction would do more to damage India than assist it. "Labour-saving" machinery would be worse than useless in a country where millions were already unable to find useful work. Industrialization was not, he felt, the right path for a nation in which 85 per cent of the population knew only a rural way of life. Improvement in the conditions of the people could only come through their own efforts in their own communities. In Gandhi's view,

> if the village perishes, India will perish too . . . . The revival of the village is possible only when it is no more exploited. Industrialization on a mass scale will necessarily lead to . . . exploitation . . . . Therefore we have to concentrate on the village being self-contained, manufacturing mainly for use.

Gandhi believed that "small is beautiful" half a century before the phrase became fashionable in the west. Big cities, big industries, big armies, big government departments all implied heavy taxes, complex regulations, and rule by experts and officials. What Gandhi wanted was "panchayat raj", a grass-roots democracy in which "we would regard the humblest and lowest Indian as being equally the ruler of India with the tallest in the land". The village community, which had survived beneath the rule of so many alien invaders, would at last emerge as the basic unit of a reformed Indian society in which each person would participate on an equal basis in the promotion of "sarvodaya" — the welfare of all.

Towards the end of his life, and despite

33 Gandhi, draped with the flag of the Republic of India, lies on his funeral pyre.

all his tremendous achievements, Gandhi regarded his career as a failure. He was horrified by the continuing violence between Muslims and Hindus, and disgusted by the ambitions of Congress politicians who, with full independence in sight, seemed to care only for power and wealth. C.R. Rajagopalacharian, a veteran nationalist leader, mused, after more than a decade of independence, on how far the country had departed from Gandhi's ideals:

What was Gandhi's wish in respect of India after it became free and the people gained the opportunity of governing themselves? He desired simplicity in living to become a general feature. He desired self-sufficiency at least in food and clothing. He desired that the citizens should govern themselves freely and that the compulsory powers of the state should be reduced to the minimum. He desired Hindus and Muslims to live in mutual trust . . . . He desired firm friendship between India and Pakistan . . . . It is painful to go through these items one by one and to realize our failures in all these respects . . .

Gandhi could not have approved the continued co-existence of great wealth and gross poverty in India, or the border wars with Pakistan, or the forcible incorporation of Hyderabad, Kashmir and Goa, or the drive for industrialization, or the possession of a nuclear bomb. But his ideas have not been completely without influence. In India, Vinoba Bhave has tried to carry through his schemes for rural development through self-help and mutual co-operation at the village level.

And the influence goes wider still. The non-aligned movement, which clearly embodies Gandhian ideals of non-violence and conciliation, has been a major contribution to international relations. And in the United States the civil rights leader Martin Luther King used Gandhian techniques of non-violent protest to immense effect in his campaign for racial equality. The importance of Gandhi and his philosophy cannot, therefore, be measured in terms of Indian history alone. Because he chose to lead a revolution not only against colonialism but also against racism, violence, poverty,

religious bigotry and economic exploitation, and because, in doing so, he gave a voice to the voiceless and power to the powerless, Gandhi must rank as a figure of world historical significance.

NEHRU

Nehru's name has become almost inseparable from that of Gandhi but, despite their close association in the nationalist movement, the two men remained very different in their outlook and philosophy.

Born in 1889, the son of a Brahmin lawyer, Jawaharial Nehru passed seven years of his youth in England, first of all at Harrow School, then at Cambridge University and at the Inner Temple, where he qualified as a barrister. Quiet and conventional in manner, he did not shine in his studies and never developed much interest in his chosen career as a lawyer. However, even as a schoolboy, Nehru had shown a passionate interest in politics although, like his father Motilal Nehru, he could find no way of fighting for the independence he believed India should have. Neither terrorist extremism, with its bomb outrages and assassinations, nor moderate constitutionalism, with its long speeches and resolutions, were acceptable to him. Gandhi, however, offered a new path, with the emphasis on action but without hatred. But, whereas, for Gandhi, non-violence was a matter of deep principle, for Nehru, it was more a convenient tactic, the method best suited to India's circumstances.

From 1919 onwards Nehru devoted himself to the Congress cause. In 1921 he became a political prisoner for the first time. Of the next twenty-four years he was to spend no fewer than nine in jail. In 1923-24 and 1927-28 he served as general secretary of Congress and in 1929 was elected president of the movement.

By this time Nehru's duties had led him to travel widely in India, giving him first-hand experience of the poverty of the peasants. He saw them as "a blind, poverty-stricken, suffering mass, resigned to their miserable fate and

exploited by all who came into contact with them''. He also made a long tour of Europe and the Soviet Union during 1926-27 and came back convinced that some form of socialism would provide the answer to India's pressing economic problems.

Nehru had become president of Congress despite the rival claims of older, more experienced politicians. This was partly a tribute to his own abilities and partly a reflection of

34   The disciple — Nehru with Gandhi.

Gandhi's concern to attach to himself and to the movement a leader, whose powerful appeal to young people and intellectuals would make him a major asset in maintaining the position of Congress as the organization to which all Indian nationalists should owe their loyalty. Nehru thus became Gandhi's political heir and was openly acknowledged as such in 1942.

35 The statesman — Nehru celebrates independence.

The price he had to pay was support for the "Quit India" movement. Nehru's own preference would have been for active Indian involvement in the war against fascism, providing India could do so as a free country.

If Gandhi was the mid-wife of India's freedom, Nehru was the nurse-maid of the newly independent nation, shaping its main policies until his death in 1964. Almost alone among the Congress leaders, he had a practical knowledge of the world beyond India. Foreign relations, therefore, became his special concern. But he was also decisive in promoting the growth of

heavy industry and economic planning by the central government. Unlike Gandhi, Nehru was less interested in reforming individuals than in building a modern nation. In his autobiography Nehru wrote:

He [Gandhi] wants people to give up bad habits and indulgences and to become pure. He lays stress on sexual abstinence, on the giving up of drink, smoking, etc. Opinions may differ about the relative wickedness of these indulgences, but . . . these personal failings are less harmful than covetousness, selfishness, acquisitiveness, the fierce conflicts of individuals for personal gain, the ruthless struggles of group and classes, the inhuman suppression and exploitation of one group by another, the terrible wars between nations.

Nehru's period of office was not without its failures, and the man himself not without his faults. But none doubted his personal sincerity, his determination to improve the condition of the poor or his commitment to democracy as a system of government. Loved in India, he was admired throughout Asia and the west and died perhaps the best-liked of twentieth-century leaders.

YOUNG HISTORIAN

A

1 Explain how Gandhi's later career was affected by the influences and events of his early life. Do the same for Nehru.

2 Why did Gandhi attach so much importance to conditions in India's villages? What did he do to improve them?

3 What did Gandhi contribute to the nationalist movement?

4 Write a dialogue between Gandhi and Nehru, showing their points of agreement and disagreement.

5 Find out about Martin Luther King and how he was influenced by Gandhi's ideas.

6 Explain the meaning of (a) ahimsa, (b) vegetarianism, (c) fasting, (d) satyagraha, (e) sadhu, (f) khadi, (g) sarvodaya.

B

Imagine you are a newspaper reporter interviewing Gandhi. What three questions would you most like to ask him? What answers do you think he would have given?

C

Write a series of headlines covering the main events in (a) Gandhi's life OR (b) Nehru's life.

D

Design a memorial which you think would be suitable for Gandhi.

INDIA SINCE INDEPENDENCE

THE STATES

Politically speaking, India faced a number of unanswered questions in 1947. One of the most pressing of these was the future of the princely states. In theory, they were free to take whatever path they chose once the British, to whom they had been bound by treaties, had left. In practice, they were tied economically to surrounding areas which were now part of independent India. It was, moreover, unthinkable to nationalists that independent India should be a mere patchwork of territory, broken up by hundreds of petty states, each claiming the right to run its own affairs. In practice, the problem proved less difficult to resolve than had been feared. Almost all of the princes joined either Pakistan or India without turmoil, in return for certain privileges, such as the continued right to use their titles and palaces, plus generous pensions. The exceptions were the Hindu ruler of Kashmir (see page 69) and the Muslim rulers of Junagadh and Hyderabad.

The ruler of Junagadh, a state on the west coast of India, north of Bombay, decided to join Pakistan, but fled when his subjects, mainly Hindus, rose in rebellion. His council invited India to take over and the people then voted overwhelmingly in favour of this decision.

The Nizam of Hyderabad, a large inland state in central India, hoped to be fully independent, but was unable, or unwilling, to resist an invasion by the Indian army in September 1948.

These developments did not complete the process of re-drawing the political map of India, however. Many small states were merged with the nearest province; the rest were grouped into five states' unions. When India's new constitution came into force in 1950, both the provinces and the states' unions became separate states of the federal republic. The constitution allowed the Indian parliament to alter state boundaries. This opened the way for different language-groups to press for a re-organization of the states, so that speakers of the same language were governed by the same state government. In 1952 a leader of the Telugu-speaking people fasted to death to protest against the refusal of the central government to create a province for Telugu-speakers. Riots accompanied his fast and followed his death. In 1953 such a state was created out of parts of Hyderabad and Mysore. Significantly, a States Re-organization Commission was established to study the overall situation. It reported in 1956 and the adoption of its recommendations made India a federation of fourteen states plus six districts especially administered by the central government (the capital, various island groups in the Indian Ocean and certain tribal areas on the Himalayan and Burmese frontiers). This re-organization served to break up the territories of some of the former princely states, such as Hyderabad, but it did not satisfy every language group. In 1960 the province of Bombay was split into Gujarat and Maharashtra, to satisfy the demands of Gujarati and Marathi speakers. In 1963 the Naga tribes of the eastern

36 Indian administrative divisions.

Himalayas, after a long campaign of resistance, obtained the status of a separate state and in 1966 the Sikhs of the eastern Punjab also achieved the status of separate statehood. In 1972 three eastern frontier areas, after a period of continued unrest, also became states.

CONGRESS AND MRS GANDHI

Throughout this period Indian politics were still dominated by the Congress party which had led the country to independence. At the state level its power was challenged by locally-based parties, especially in the south. The Communists and their allies even took over in Kerala in 1957 and in West Bengal in 1967. But opposition parties rarely won two elections in succession. Whenever the Congress lost an election, its leaders would end their rivalries and concentrate on dividing their opponents.

National, as opposed to state-level, politics remained firmly in the hands of Congress. When Nehru died in 1964, Congress chose as his successor Lal Bahadur Shastri. When he died suddenly in January 1966, Congress chose Indira Gandhi, the daughter of Jawaharlal Nehru.

The nation's fourth general election was held in 1967. The Congress majority in parliament fell and the party lost control of all but eight of the seventeen state governments. Not surprisingly, some of the Congress politicians blamed the new leader. The Party split in 1969, one wing supporting Mrs Gandhi and the other opposing her. In the 1971 election Mrs Gandhi's opponents were united only by their slogan "Indira Hatao" (get rid of Indira). Her supporters fought on the slogan "Gharib Hatao" (get rid of poverty) and won an overwhelming victory, carrying two thirds of the seats in the lower house of parliament. This popular support enabled Mrs Gandhi to press forward with plans to provide better credit for farmers and small businessmen and to end the pensions paid to

37 Mrs Indira Gandhi photographed distributing relief aid in Orissa in 1966.

former princes. Her popularity was further increased as a result of India's successful military intervention on behalf of Bangladesh. When elections were held at state level in 1972, Congress won 16 out of the 20 contests.

Mrs Gandhi's opponents, whether former rivals in the Congress or members of other parties, had not, however, given up hope of breaking her power. Gathering around J.P. Narayan, a respected veteran politician, they started a Gandhian style non-cooperation movement, accusing Mrs Gandhi of corruption and abuse of her powers. The impact of the 1973 oil-price rise led to rapid inflation, strikes, smuggling and general discontent — a perfect background for agitation against a hard-pressed government. In June 1975 the High Court found Mrs Gandhi guilty of corrupt practices in the 1971 general elections. (It had been alleged, for instance, that she used official planes and jeeps to help the campaign of her political supporters, while her opponents had to pay for their own transport.) She was disqualified from holding elected office for a period of six years and her opponents organized a march on Delhi to demand her immediate resignation.

STATE OF EMERGENCY

At this critical point many experienced political observers, both within India and abroad, were sympathetic towards Mrs Gandhi. She had been convicted on a legal technicality and the sentence passed upon her seemed rather severe. It was more than possible that, upon appeal, the Supreme Court might have annulled it altogether. Mrs Gandhi might have resigned with honour and later returned to power in triumph. But she did not. Fearing, perhaps, that, if she once left office, her opponents would ensure that she would never regain it, that they might well pack the Supreme Court with hostile judges, or make new charges against her, she decided to confront them. Using her powers as President, Mrs Gandhi declared an official State of Emergency on 26 June 1975. Nine hundred of her leading opponents were impri-

soned, a number of political groups were banned, strict censorship was introduced and the sixth general election, due to be held in March 1976, was postponed for one year. In November the Supreme Court upheld Mrs Gandhi's appeal against her conviction on charges of corrupt election practices. In December it was announced that the State of Emergency would continue and that elections would be postponed until 1978.

Meanwhile Mrs Gandhi had announced a programme of radical reforms and tough policies to ensure their enforcement. Emergency regulations gave the government sweeping powers which brought strikes to an end, slowed down the rise in prices and obliged officials to get to work on time. Ruling as a virtual dictator, Mrs Gandhi entrusted more and more power to a small group of trusted personal advisers, and notably to her son Sanjay, leader of the all-India Youth Congress. Under Sanjay's direction, tens of thousands of squatter shanties around Delhi were bulldozed, and the birth control programme was pressed forward by pressurizing men with more than three children to accept sterilization "voluntarily". Both Sanjay and his older brother Rajiv were also involved in shady business deals which broke official regulations on imports.

THE FALL AND COME-BACK OF MRS GANDHI

Support for Mrs Gandhi was widespread, however, among the better-off, and especially among businessmen. In February 1977 she suddenly announced that elections would be held in the following month. Her motives for this decision to let the people pass judgement on her government are still not clear. As it turned out, the decision was a political disaster. Most of her opponents united together in a single organization, the Janata Party, under Morarji Desai. Jagjivan Ram, the veteran Congress leader who had supported Mrs Gandhi throughout the Emergency, set up his own group, the Congress for Democracy (CFD). When the votes were

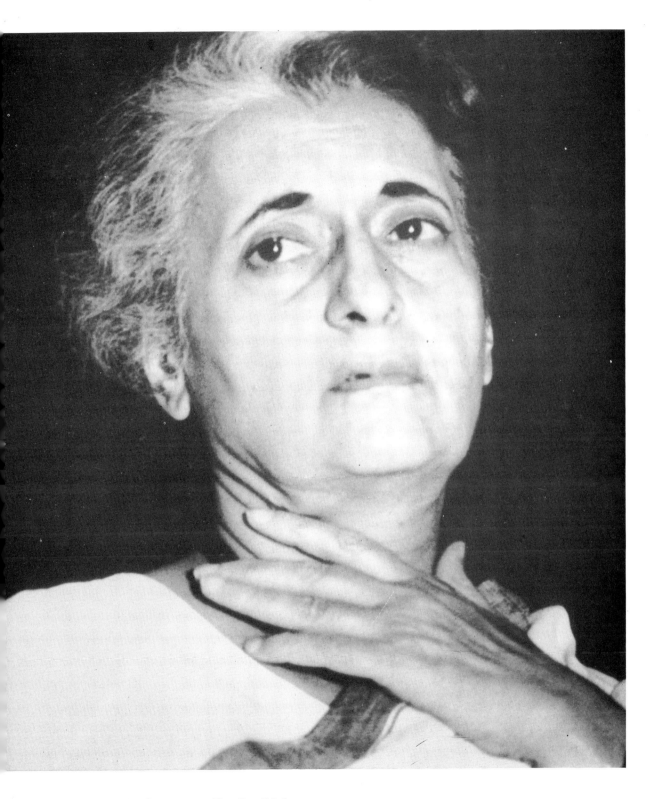

38 Not yet the end of an era — Mrs Gandhi faces
defeat in the 1977 election.

counted, Janata was shown to have won 270 seats and the CFD 29, to Mrs Gandhi's 153. Mrs Gandhi lost her own seat by a margin of more than 50,000 votes. She accepted the entire blame for her party's performance and left office without hesitation.

The new government, under Morarji Desai, appointed a commission of enquiry under a former Chief Justice, J.E. Shah, to investigate the conduct of Mrs Gandhi's government during the Emergency. While the commission sat, Mrs Gandhi went about preparing for her come-back, splitting the Congress Party in January 1978 to form a new "Indira Congress" under her personal leadership. In February this new faction was popular enough to win outright majorities in the state elections of Karnataka and Andhra Pradesh. In March and April 1978 interim reports of the Shah Commission found Mrs Gandhi guilty of corruption and abuse of power. Desai's reluctance to act against Mrs

Gandhi led to a growing split in the Janata party. In November a sitting MP in the new Indira Congress stronghold of Karnataka obligingly resigned and Mrs Gandhi took over his seat in the ensuing by-election. In December, however, parliament found her guilty of breach of privilege during the Emergency and expelled her. Her brief imprisonment led to widespread riots and demonstrations in her support.

In the summer of 1979 the Desai government finally broke up and was succeeded by a brief caretaker administration under Charan Singh. The general election of January 1980 saw Mrs Gandhi swept back to power, with a two thirds majority, in the most remarkable political come-back in the modern history of India.

39 Mrs Gandhi as the Goddess of Destruction — an unflattering opposition portrait during the 1980 election.

40 On the winning side — supporters of Mrs Gandhi
parade through a provincial city to rally votes (1980).

YOUNG HISTORIAN

A

1 Describe how India has been re-organized politically since 1947.
2 Why have language problems been so important in Indian politics?
3 What problems arise for India as a democracy, from the fact that most of the adult population is illiterate?
4 Explain the meaning of (a) federation, (b) state of emergency.

B

Imagine you are a reporter going to interview Mrs Gandhi. What three questions would you choose to ask and why?

C

Write a series of headlines outlining the career of Mrs Gandhi since 1966.

D

Design an election poster either in support of Mrs Gandhi or against her.

67

INDIA'S FOREIGN POLICY

ATOMIC POWER

In May 1974 India successfully exploded an atomic "device" and thus became the sixth nation in the world to have the status of a nuclear power. Many people, both inside India and abroad, criticized the vast expenditures involved in India's atomic programme; but the government argued that atomic weapons were essential to preserve India's independence and that atomic power could also be used for peaceful purposes in the economic development of the nation.

NON-ALIGNMENT

India's foreign policy has been based partly on commitments inherited from the British Raj (in particular, a concern to control the Himalayan regions which divide Indian territory from that of neighbouring superpower, China) and partly on the principle of "non-alignment" inherited from the Congress, largely under Nehru's inspiration. As Prime Minister from 1947 to 1964, Nehru also took the main responsibility for India's foreign affairs, being the only nationalist politician with any great experience of the wider world beyond India. Nehru hoped that India's foreign policy could combine a realistic concern with her own national interests, in terms of defence and development, with a genuine desire to assist other nations against poverty, colonial rule and racial injustice. "Non-alignment", as Nehru explained it, would not mean isolation from world affairs, which would, in any case, have been impossible for a nation as large as India. Nor would it mean a refusal to take initiatives or to take sides. Ideally, non-alignment would mean a pragmatic policy of judging each international issue on its merits and steadfastly refusing to commit India in advance to the support of any single state or group of states, and especially the USA and USSR.

During the 1950s the idea of "non-alignment" had a powerful appeal for the leaders and peoples of other newly independent states in Asia and Africa. This was strengthened by India's willingness to contribute troops to UN peace-keeping forces in Korea, Indo-China, the Congo and Cyprus. On the other hand, India's forceful take-over of the Portuguese colony of Goa in 1961 showed that she was still willing to use military power to settle international disputes to her own advantage. And her defeat at the hands of China in 1962 (see page 72) led to a severe, if temporary, loss of prestige. The lessening of tension between the USA and the USSR in the 1960s gave India less opportunity to step forward as mediator or spokesman of the middle way. And after Nehru's death his successors were more and more concerned with India's pressing domestic problems than with exerting a major influence in world affairs.

PAKISTAN

India's most persisting problems in foreign policy have concerned her relations with neighbouring Pakistan. Partition left a legacy of bitterness and began a process of refugee movement between the two countries which never entirely stopped, even when they were on relatively good terms with each other.

The first major crisis between India and Pakistan arose over the fate of the Himalayan kingdom of Kashmir. In 1947 its population was about three quarters Muslim, but its ruler, a Hindu, refused to join either India or Pakistan. Pakistan tried to force the issue by supporting Pakistani hill-peoples in an invasion of Kashmir. When the Maharajah of Kashmir appealed to India for military assistance, it was given, on

condition that Kashmir would join India; it was also agreed that, once order had been re-established, the people of Kashmir would be allowed to vote on the future of their country. In 1949 the UN arranged a cease-fire in Kashmir. One third of the country was by then under the control of the Pakistani Azad (Free) Kashmir government. Negotiations between India and Pakistan failed to resolve the issue of control, and the cease-fire line became, in effect, a frontier between the two parts of a partitioned country. In 1956 a locally elected assembly in Kashmir adopted a constitution which declared that the "State of Jammu and Kashmir is and shall be an integral part of the Union of India".

Unrest in Kashmir and incidents along the cease-fire line encouraged further pressure from Pakistan in 1965. In April an armed clash took place in the disputed Rann of Kutch, an area of desert and marsh in Gujarat, potentially rich

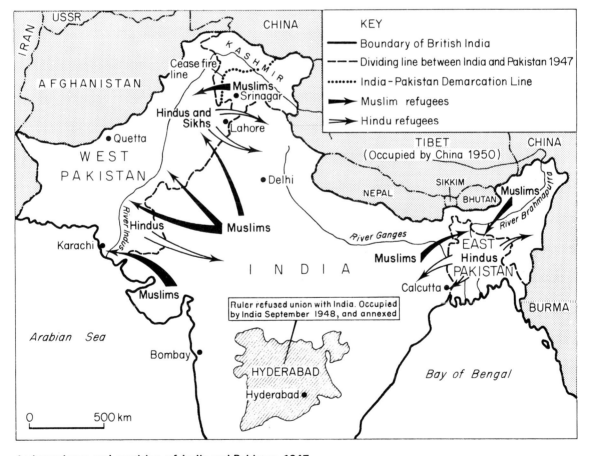

41   Independence and partition of India and Pakistan, 1947.

in oil. In June the two sides agreed to withdraw from the contested region and to accept arbitration. While this issue was shelved, however, the situation in Kashmir was once again inflamed by the operations of Pakistan-trained guerillas, followed by the movement of Pakistani armoured units into Jammu. India, in retaliation, launched an attack across the Punjab towards Lahore. The US and Britain cut off arms supplies to both sides and got the UN Security Council to call for a cease-fire, which was accepted in September. At this point the USSR offered to mediate, and at Tashkent in January 1966 both sides agreed to withdraw to their pre-war positions. India gained nothing from the conflict, but the success of her army restored her confidence, which had been badly dented by failure against China in 1962 (see page 72). In 1968 she also accepted the judgement of an arbitration commission which awarded Pakistan about one tenth of the disputed Rann of Kutch.

Growing unrest in East Pakistan in 1971 led to frequent border clashes between Indian and Pakistani frontier-guards trying respectively to protect and to pursue Bengali guerillas using Indian territory as a sanctuary. When, on 3 December, Pakistan tried to knock out a number of Indian air bases, India struck back in both the east and the west. By 16 December Indian troops had entered Dacca and accepted the surrender of Pakistan's forces. This armed intervention of India in support of the independence of Bangladesh (see page 86) helped to ensure the return of the 10 million refugees who had fled into her territory and whose relief had become a major burden. The war also demonstrated convincingly that India was the undisputed major power in the South Asian region. However, India still regards Pakistan as a threat to its security.

The military element in Pakistan's government remains strong and foreign policy may reasonably be supposed, therefore, to be made in terms of military objectives. There is Pakistan's long-standing friendship with China and her growing links, through the common bond of Islam, with the newly-powerful oil states of the Arab world. And there is still the irritant of Kashmir.

INDIA'S OTHER NEIGHBOURS

India's relations with her other neighbours have not been without problems. The conditions of the million-strong Tamil minority in Sri Lanka (a legacy of the migration of Tamil plantation-workers from southern India during the colonial period) has continued to cause concern in India.

The Himalayan kingdoms of Nepal, Sikkim and Bhutan have, by contrast, raised problems of security rather than of social injustice. Nepal's "complete sovereignty" was recognized by India in 1950 and has been preserved by a skilful balancing act, whereby the country receives aid from both India and China, the USA and the USSR. Sikkim, until 1974 a protectorate of India, has since been accorded "associate" status within the Indian Union. In practice, India controls its foreign policy and defence and is taking an increasing interest in its internal affairs. China, however, continues to acknowledge the "separate identity and political status" of Sikkim. Bhutan, the most isolated of the three Himalayan states, agreed in 1949 "to be guided" by Indian advice on foreign relations. While India provides an annual subsidy to its government, it has chosen not to intervene in its domestic affairs.

CHINA

India's concern to uphold the British tradition of regarding the Himalayas as a buffer zone brought her into conflict with China over the status of Tibet. India wanted to see Tibet independent, but in 1954 Nehru, determined to improve relations with the People's Republic of China, recognized it as a "region of China". In 1959, however, a mass rising in Tibet against Chinese influence led to confrontation between India and China. China claimed some 40,000 square miles of Indian territory which, in China's eyes, had been unjustly taken from her during the period of British rule. Among the claimed areas were practically the whole of the North East Frontier Province (usually known as NEFA and now called Ammachal Pradesh) and the Aksai Chin, a vast desolate plain in Kashmir, across which in 1957 the Chinese had completed an all-weather road to link Tibet with their westernmost province of Sinkiang, itself exposed to Russian pressure. The road was discovered by Indian patrols in 1958 and its existence was made generally known to the Indian public in 1959 when the Tibetan revolt led to frontier clashes in the region.

In 1960 China offered to give up her claims in NEFA in return for the Aksai Chin, which she already controlled. India, however, was determined to yield no territory. Therefore, on 20 October 1962, China invaded NEFA with the object of forcing India back to the negotiating table. Ignoring the offer of a cease-fire and fresh discussions, India decided to resist the Chinese invasion. Within a month Chinese troops, far better trained and equipped than their Indian counter-parts for cold mountain fighting, had pushed 150 miles into NEFA territory. On 20 November China announced a cease-fire and voluntarily withdrew her forces to the 1959 "line of actual control". She remains in possession of the Aksai Chin.

THE USA AND THE USSR

India's relations with the USA have been troubled by American support for Pakistan. America's aim was to create a cordon of military allies between the USSR and the oil-fields of the Middle East. This involved building up the armed strength of Pakistan. Despite assurances that American weapons supplied to Pakistan for defence against Russia would never be used against India, the United States was not, in fact, able to prevent this from happening. American support for Pakistan in her suppression of the nationalist movement in Bangladesh also worsened relations with India. On the other hand, India has accepted substantial amounts of foreign aid from America, and notably large stocks of grain, amounting in the 1960s to some one quarter of the American wheat crop.

Russia, by contrast, has viewed India since the 1950s as a vital counter-weight to China and has sought to assure her friendship through economic assistance (e.g. building the Bhilai steel-works), military aid (the first Indian-built MIG fighters were completed in 1968) and diplomatic support (e.g. for the Indian position over Kashmir and Goa).

Despite the value India places on the Soviet connection, she continues to seek self-reliance in international affairs. Skilful diplomacy can release her from dependence on any one power. Her continuing need to import energy, food and advanced technology ensures, however, that self-reliance can only be achieved through cooperation with others.

YOUNG HISTORIAN

A

1 Explain why you do or do not agree with India's policy of becoming a nuclear power.
2 Why have India and Pakistan had so many disputes with each other since they became independent?
3 Why has India generally been on better terms with the USSR than with China?
4 Explain the meaning of (a) non-alignment, (b) isolation, (c) cease-fire, (d) arbitration, (e) mediate, (f) sovereignty, (g) subsidy, (h) buffer zone.

B

Imagine you are either (a) an officer in the Indian army or (b) an Indian journalist. Write an account of your experiences during any two of the conflicts described in this chapter.

C

Write a series of headlines covering the main events in India's external affairs since 1947.

D

Draw a map of South Asia and mark in the areas where India has been involved in disputes with her neighbours.

INDIA AS A DEVELOPING COUNTRY

Writing in the mid-1930s, Nehru saw India as:

a servile State, with its splendid strength caged up, hardly daring to breathe freely, governed by strangers from afar; her people poor beyond compare, short-lived and incapable of resisting disease and epidemic; illiteracy rampant; vast areas devoid of all sanitary or medical provision; unemployment on a prodigious scale . . .

He conceded that a certain amount of economic progress had taken place during the period of British rule, but thought that little credit for this could be given to the British:

Railways, telegraphs, telephones, wireless and the like were not tests of the goodness or beneficence of British rule. They were welcome and necessary and because the British happened to be the agents who brought them first, we should be grateful to them. But even these heralds of industrialism came to us primarily for the strengthening of British rule. . .

When India became independent, Nehru, therefore, gave a high priority to the task of economic development. An admirer of Soviet achievements — though not of the harsh methods used in Russia — he authorized the adoption of a policy of central planning, by which the government would modernize the economy by coordinating investment, taxation, training, trade, etc, through a series of Five Year Plans. These would set the overall goals for the economy and select the projects necessary to realize them. The planning process is complicated by the fact that policies affecting agriculture, health and education are made at state level and the states, therefore, have to be consulted. And, because India (unlike China) is a "mixed economy", with a large private sector outside direct government control, carrying out the plans involves gaining the cooperation of businessmen through incentives, rather than ordering it via directives.

INDUSTRY

In the early Five Year Plans emphasis was given to the building-up of industry. India was already a major steel producer before independence and is fortunate in having large deposits of high-grade iron ore. (She also has manganese and bauxite, uranium, coal, and petroleum.) India is now one of the world's largest steel producers.

Indian steel is cheap and much goes for export, but the bulk is absorbed by the wide range of manufacturing industries which have developed since independence. India is the world's largest producer of railway wagons and also produces such goods as tractors, diesel engines, heavy electrical gear, and artificial fertilizers.

43 Two technologies side by side — cooling towers and bamboo ladders at the Durgapur steel project.

44 Saris at the workbench. Does India need a female labour force in industry? Do Indian women need employment?

45 Basic technology — a stick and a stone wheel serve this village potter.

The development of large-scale industry employing modern technology has enabled India to provide most of the weapons for her army (the fourth largest in the world), to supply the needs of the construction and transport sectors for machinery, and to cater for the tastes of the better-off town-dwellers, as well as to earn foreign exchange through the export of manufactures, especially textiles. But large-scale industry employs only about five million people, and India desperately needs to create employment and to produce goods cheaply for rural consumers with low incomes. For this reason small-scale industry, employing simpler technology, and traditional handicrafts, calling upon established skills, have been encouraged since the 1970s. This, in a sense, represents a swing back to the Gandhian idea of putting the needs of men before the appetites of machines.

India's industrial growth has been impressive. Industrial output tripled between 1951 and 1971.

AGRICULTURE

But India is essentially an agricultural country with four fifths of her population living in rural areas. Of the nation's 327 million hectares about 142 million are under cultivation and very little of what remains is suitable for agriculture. Over 80 per cent of the cropped area is used for growing food grains (especially rice and wheat), mainly for subsistence rather than for sale.

77

The most pressing need is to expand the food supply while creating employment. Many difficulties stand in the way:

(a) reliance on monsoon rains makes farmers vulnerable to drought and flood. Only one quarter of India's arable land is irrigated and investment in irrigation is expensive.

(b) cash crops (tea, jute, spices) account for one third of exports and take up some of the best land and managers.

(c) Three quarters of all land-holdings are less than three hectares in size; these account for one third of the cultivated area. Many peasants cannot grow enough to feed their families and are forced into debt.

46 Transplanting rice, a labour-intensive task.

During the late 1960s the so-called "Green Revolution" led to large increases in output in the Punjab and Haryana. This "Green Revolution" depended upon the introduction of new high-yielding varieties of wheat and rice. But the high yields could only be obtained if the "miracle seed" was treated with the appropriate fertilizers and pesticides and assured of a good water supply. The better-off land-owners could afford these additional costs or were able to borrow money on credit, and, therefore, they benefited most. Smaller farmers, unable to compete, were often obliged to sell off their land. Between 1961 and 1971 the number of landless labourers rose by 81 per cent, from

17.3 million to 31.3 million. Laws to limit the accumulation of good-quality land by richer farmers were widely evaded as land-owners sought to take advantage of the new opportunities available to them. On the other hand, by 1977 there were 18 million tonnes of food in stock, enough to tide the country over two successive bad monsoons.

ACHIEVEMENTS OF THE FIVE YEAR PLANS

Efforts to build up India's economy have often been disrupted by political problems or harvest failures. During the First Five Year Plan (1951-

47 Lining an irrigation canal to prevent water loss through seepage. Such projects prevent waste but take years to pay off their costs.

56) India benefited from the Korean War boom in world trade which raised the price of its exports, but the ending of this boom brought a fall in export earnings, at the same time as three years of drought forced the government to import grain from abroad. The 1962 war likewise forced the government to double its military spending. This was followed by further spending on the 1965 war, more severe droughts in 1966 and 1967 and more war expenditure in 1971. For these reasons the second, third and fourth Plans all failed to reach the targets they had set.

48 The spelling is eccentric but the message is clear in this 1947 poster.

49 Government bulk purchase of grain — controlling prices and distribution are as important as raising production.

Economic progress has not been made evenly throughout the country. In the west and south food grain production has risen considerably faster than the population, but in the east, especially in West Bengal, Assam, Bihar and Orissa, the reverse has been the case. By 1971 every village in Haryana had electricity, while less than 10 per cent had in Bihar. In the Punjab 70 per cent of the land was irrigated, in West Bengal only 22 per cent. Nor have the fruits of progress been evenly distributed. The poorest 30 per cent of the population account for less than 15 per cent of private consumption. An estimated 8 million Indians suffer from tuberculosis and 14 out of every 1,000 suffer from total or partial blindness. There are only 100,000 doctors to serve the needs of more than 600 million people, and the illiteracy rate is still around 70 per cent.

In some respects, the drive for national improvement is losing rather than gaining ground. In 1965 there were 100,000 cases of malaria reported, in 1975 4,500,000. Food supply, employment opportunities and basic health and education services cannot be expanded fast enough to keep up with the massive growth in population, which increases by about 15 million each year — an increase larger than the total population of Australia or of Greater London. Between 1974 and 1989 an estimated 65 million people will be added to the labour force — 3½ times as many as are currently working in paid employment.

Vigorous family planning programmes have been carried out but have failed either to reach or to convince many millions in slums and rural areas. Where there is no social security, a large family is still the best insurance for one's old age. While the population continues to expand rapidly, the Indian economy must run to stand still. The draft of the Fifth Five Year Plan opened with the words "Removal of poverty and attainment of economic self-reliance are the two strategic goals that the country has set for itself". These were essentially the goals that were set in 1947. They are far from being attained.

YOUNG HISTORIAN

A

1 How far has independent India developed in ways of which Gandhi would have approved?

2 Why is agriculture so important for India? How has it been improved? How could it be further improved?

3 How has India's economic development been affected by political events?

4 Why has economic improvement not occurred at the same rate and to the same extent in different parts of India?

5 Find out how India has been affected by rising oil prices.

6 Explain the meaning of (a) epidemic, (b) central planning, (c) mixed economy, (d) foreign exchange, (e) subsistence, (f) social security, (g) family planning.

B

"A small family is a happy family" is one of the slogans used by the family planning campaign in India. Make up a series of slogans to support campaigns for education, clean water, more nutritious food and basic health care methods.

C

Write a short paragraph about the importance of each of the following industries in modern India: (a) steel, (b) film-making, (c) textiles.

D

Draw a map and mark in some of the main examples of India's economic progress since independence.

PAKISTAN AND BANGLADESH

THE EFFECTS OF PARTITION

Partition created grave difficulties both for India and for Pakistan. But for Pakistan the legacies of partition were to prove both more burdensome and more enduring. Whereas India was based on a single territorial unit, whose varying regions were at least connected by its great railway network, Pakistan was divided into two quite distinct portions, more than a thousand miles apart, which, therefore, relied heavily on sea and air routes for communication.

And, whereas India contained all four of the greatest cities of the whole South Asian region — Delhi, Calcutta, Madras and Bombay — Pakistan had only one major cultural and economic centre, Lahore. Neither Karachi in the west, nor Dacca in the east of Pakistan had ever been more than centres of merely provincial importance.

Both India and Pakistan had to cope with about six million refugees in the first year of independence. For India, the refugee problem meant aiding and resettling an additional one sixtieth of her population; for Pakistan, the refugees represented a proportion almost four times as great. And, while most of the Muslims who fled to Pakistan were village labourers, a large proportion of the Hindus who sought safety in India were professional men, traders and skilled artisans. Their expertise, which was to prove a bonus for India, was lost to Pakistan. Pakistan's crippling shortage of skills is well illustrated by the fact that she was obliged to recruit large numbers of British officials, former members of the Indian Civil Service, to staff her administration.

Economically too, the two states presented a stark contrast. India inherited the vast majority of the region's modern factories and 95 per cent of its established hydro-electric plant. Pakistan, which grew virtually all the world's supply of jute, had not a single mill after partition with which to process it.

The strain of independence soon took its toll in politics. Muhammad Ali Jinnah, founder of Pakistan and its first governor-general, died of a heart attack in September 1948. He was succeeded by Liaqat Ali Khan, his long-time lieutenant. But whereas the assassination of Gandhi shocked Indians into a sort of unity, which ended anti-Muslim riots, the death of Jinnah left the people of Pakistan feeling that they had lost not just their leader but their sense of direction as well. And while Nehru was to rule India for some sixteen years after the death of Gandhi, Liaqat Ali Khan was to be assassinated in 1951.

Pakistan had been created as a state for Muslims; but, apart from the fact that it was split in two physically, and still contained some ten million Hindus, it was also divided in other ways and chiefly by language. East Pakistan (the former East Bengal) had more than half of the state's total population and spoke Bengali; in West Pakistan the main language was Urdu, but others were also important. In an attempt to promote national unity, the lands of the once semi-independent frontier chieftains who had opted to join Pakistan were merged together to form the provinces of Baluchistan and the North West Frontier. In 1955 these were united with West Punjab and Sind to form a single province, West Pakistan. This led, however, to difficult relations with Pakistan's neighbour, Afghanistan. When leaders of the frontier tribes began to demand a return to their former autonomy, it was suggested that there should be an independent state of "Pushtunistan" for the tribes which shared the Pushtu language with many of their Afghan neighbours. In 1969 West Pakistan was again divided into four provinces. It was, however, the continuing rivalry between Urdu and Bengali which was to lead to the eventual break-up of the state.

THE CONSTITUTION

The political life of Pakistan since independence has revolved largely around the problem of devising a system of government which could prove to be both effective in developing the country and acceptable to the vast majority of its inhabitants. In 1947 Pakistan, like India, established itself as a federal republic, acknowledging the British crown only as a symbol of the unity of the Commonwealth. Like India also, Pakistan retained the parliamentary form of government and gave more power to the central government than to those of the various provinces. But, while India was able to put its constitution into full effect in 1950, the constituent assembly of Pakistan in the same year refused to approve the draft presented to it. Bengali members of the assembly thought it placed East Pakistan too firmly under the hand of the central government, which was based in West Pakistan. And prominent Muslims thought it paid too little heed to the requirements of Islam, which had been supposed to be the very reason for which Pakistan should exist as a separate state. Eventually a constitution was accepted in 1956. No attempt was to be made to establish a single national language. A good deal of autonomy was to be given to East Pakistan.

And the laws of the state were to be brought into harmony with the Sharia, the laws of Islam based on the Qur'an and the sayings and deeds of the prophet Muhammad. The problems were, however, far from being solved. Autonomy in Bengal became the basis for a full-blown independence movement. It proved extremely difficult to revise the laws to harmonize with Islam, because the experts could not agree amongst themselves about what Islam required. And the constitution itself was replaced by another in 1962, which was itself to be replaced in 1969 and that in turn was replaced in 1973.

LEADERS OF PAKISTAN

Effective government depends largely upon effective leadership, that is, leadership which is both competent and trusted. In Pakistan such leadership seems to have been difficult to establish in power. Few of the leaders of the nationalist movement had any experience to match that of their counterparts in India, many of whom had served in provincial governments during the period of dyarchy (see page 37). The real demand for a separate Pakistan had come only seven years before the state had been formed and, right up to the moment of its establishment, its future leaders had been more concerned to argue the case for its existence than to make detailed plans for its actual running.

The sudden deaths of Jinnah and Liaqat Ali Khan deprived the Muslim League of the personalities on which its appeal had largely been based. In 1954 the League went down to defeat before a coalition of opposition parties in the provincial elections in East Pakistan. In 1956 it was defeated in West Pakistan.

Meanwhile, the short-staffed civil service, many of whose members regarded themselves as over-worked and under-paid, began to abuse its authority and to become a prey to corruption. In 1958 the president of the republic asked Muhammad Ayub Khan, the commander-in-chief of the armed forces, to take over the country

50 Opposition Muslim League protesters felled by tear-gas (1958).

and stamp out corruption. Ayub Khan suspended the constitution, abolished political parties and relied heavily on the army to provide him with the trained and educated manpower needed to manage the affairs of a nation committed to rapid development.

MUHAMMAD AYUB KHAN

Under Ayub Khan, corruption was cut down and, as if to mark a fresh start in the life of the nation, it was decided to move the seat of government from Karachi to a brand new capital, Islamabad, to be built in the north, nearer to the unsettled frontier areas. In 1960 a system of "basic democracy" was introduced.

This allowed people to vote for their local council, which in turn elected the members of the district council and so on, up to the regional, provincial and national levels. All councils above the local level included officials appointed by the government and these non-elected members tended to dominate both discussion and decision-making. Representatives elected by this system made Ayub Khan president for a five-year term and accepted the 1962 constitution, based on the "basic democracy" system, which made the cabinet, the supreme decision-making body of the nation, dependent on the approval of the president rather than on that of the legislature. The legislature was re-sited in Dacca. On the one hand, this may show that Ayub Khan was concerned to soothe Bengali feelings of resentment at the domination of the government by Urdu speakers. On the other hand, it may also show that the legislature was to have so little serious power that it scarcely mattered whether it met

51   Ayub Khan visits Sri Lanka.

a thousand miles away from the nerve centres of government or not.

Ayub Khan hoped to govern without political parties, but soon found that he needed some sort of party to organize his supporters in the legislature and that former politicians would not accept a permanent ban on political activity. In 1962 parties were once again permitted. Ayub Khan survived their challenge and re-emerged as president in 1965, but he found himself increasingly beset by problems arising from the economic inequalities within the nation — the great gulf between the poverty of the ordinary villagers and the wealth of the "twenty-two families" who were alleged to own two thirds of the nation's industry — and also by the growing gap between West Pakistan, where most of the new economic development was taking place, and East Pakistan, where most of the nation's exports were produced and the larger portion of the nation's population were struggling to maintain a very basic standard of living.

THE CREATION OF BANGLADESH

In 1966 Sheikh Mujibur Rahman, leader of the Awami League in East Pakistan, demanded that the province should have much more independence from the central government. As a result, he was accused of treason and imprisoned. Protests against the government led to his release and demands for a new constitution. In West Pakistan discontent was also growing. In 1967 Zulfikar Ali Bhutto, a former foreign minister, was imprisoned for criticizing the government. Finally, riots led to the resignation of Ayub Khan in 1969. The chief of staff of the armed forces, Muhammad Yahya Khan, took over and called elections to choose a constituent assembly which would draw up a new constitution. In the East the Awami League won 160 of the 162 seats; in the West Bhutto's Pakistan "People's Party" won 81 out of 138 seats. Critics of the government clearly had widespread popular support. But the constituent assembly never met, because Yahya Khan

refused to accept the Awami League's proposals as a starting-point for debate. The League, therefore, under Sheikh Mujib, proclaimed East Pakistan to be the independent state of Bangladesh ("Free Bengal").

For eight months the Pakistan army tried to suppress the Mukti Bahini, a guerilla force of Bengalis fighting in support of Sheikh Mujib. Military intervention by India led swiftly to the surrender of the Pakistan army and the resignation of Yahya Khan. Bhutto, as the leader of the largest political grouping in the West became ruler of the new Pakistan, now reduced to its western provinces.

PAKISTAN UNDER BHUTTO

Bhutto, Pakistan's first democratically elected prime minister, inherited a state on the verge of collapse. He soon showed himself to be a skilled and ruthless political leader, as arrogant as he was able. He successfully negotiated with India the return of 90,000 Pakistani prisoners of war and the evacuation of 6,000 square miles of captured territory. In 1972 he took Pakistan out of the Commonwealth in protest against the general recognition among its members of the independence of Bangladesh. In 1974, however, the independence of Bangladesh was at last recognized by Pakistan. At home Bhutto challenged the power of the great industrialists and took over a number of the largest firms owned by the "22 families". Twelve hundred officials were sacked from the civil service on charges of corruption and a number of senior army officers were removed from their positions.

Having established himself securely in power, Bhutto continued to strengthen his position by using a newly-established para-military organization, the Federal Security Force, to harass his political opponents. Critics of his government were imprisoned and beaten up. A personality cult was promoted, with Bhutto's picture appearing in public buildings alongside that of Jinnah. Parks and polo tournaments were named in his honour. Many of his former supporters, particularly the students and intell-

52 Bangladesh freedom-fighters — most were not so
well-armed.

ectuals, became disenchanted with his rule.
His repressive methods were feared and his
reforms in favour of greater economic justice
did not seem to many to go far enough.

The authority of the central government was,
moreover, threatened by unrest in frontier
areas. Fighting between tribal guerillas and
government forces continued intermittently
from 1973 to 1976 in Baluchistan. In 1975
a Pushtunistan separatist movement became
active in the North West Frontier Province.
The National Awami Party (NAP) was banned
for allegedly directing terrorist activities and
aiming to break up the state.

In March 1977 elections were held for the
national and provincial assemblies. The NAP
was barred from taking part but nine opposition parties joined together as the Pakistan
National Alliance (PNA) to oppose the Pakistan
People's Party (PPP). When the PPP won 155
of the 200 seats in the national assembly,
Bhutto claimed the overwhelming victory he

had so confidently expected. Riots followed,
however, when the opposition claimed that the
whole election had been rigged. Bhutto had
certainly rigged previous by-elections and this
was enough to make a charge of general ballot-
rigging seem credible to many who had cause
to resent Bhutto's rule. (In fact, a later commission of enquiry was able to uncover only
isolated instances of unfair election practices.)

THE OVERTHROW OF BHUTTO

Bhutto was forced to call in the military to
restore order, and martial law was imposed
in several cities. Realizing that Bhutto had
forfeited his earlier popularity, the army over-
threw him in July 1977, suspending the constitution and establishing General Mohammad
Zia ul-Haq, the army Chief of Staff, as Chief
Martial Law Administrator. In September
Bhutto was arrested on a charge of having
ordered the murder of the father of a former

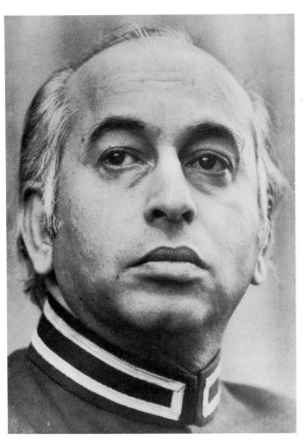

53 Zulfikar Ali Bhutto — politician, patriot and martyr?

political opponent. Later he was also charged with corruption, treason, abduction and contempt of court. In March 1978 Bhutto was sentenced to death for conspiracy to murder. He was hanged in April 1979, despite worldwide pleas for mercy.

ISLAM

General Zia, who took over the office of President in September 1978, emphasized the Islamic character of his government, and stern punishments were imposed on offenders against Islamic law.

54 PPP followers mourn Bhutto on the day of his execution.

Ties with Muslim countries in the Middle East and Africa, who supply Pakistan with much-needed foreign aid, have been strengthened. Although various civilian politicians have been brought into the government from time to time, General Zia announced in 1979 that the elections which had long been promised would not be held until he was satisfied that corruption had been stamped out and the economy had been put on a sounder footing.

55 General Zia of Pakistan.

ECONOMY

Pakistan's economic development has undoubtedly been slowed down by the strains of war and the uncertainties which accompany civil unrest and political instability. Land still remains very unevenly distributed, in spite of reforms. Mineral and energy resources exist

56 Demonstrators celebrate the introduction of Islamic laws.

but have not yet been greatly developed. Adult literacy is still only 15 per cent and more than half of the children in the country do not go to school, although free primary education is a constitutional right. Fulfilment of the government's ambitious plans for increasing food supplies, improving communications, promoting industry and spreading better social services into rural areas depends essentially on the creation of a regime which is both effective and widely supported.

THE HISTORY OF BANGLADESH

The same, of course, can be said of Bangladesh, whose short history has been equally troubled. Revolutions change governments, not geography. Whether it is called East Pakistan or Bangladesh, it remains a small country (56,000 square miles)

57 Sheikh Mujibur Rahman.

with a large population (more than 80 million) and very few natural resources, having little building stone and no iron ore. It is also especially vulnerable to floods and cyclones. About 40 per cent of the labour force is either under-employed or completely unemployed. And each year the population grows by about 3 per cent, despite the fact that one baby in seven dies within a year of its birth. Foreign aid at the rate of some $1,500 million a year has helped to keep the country going. But the attack on poverty has scarcely begun to take effect. And, meanwhile, the population continues to rise. In the face of these difficulties, Bangladesh, like Pakistan, has turned to military rule — and another General Zia.

Although Sheikh Mujib won a convincing victory in the elections of March 1973, the authority of his government was immediately threatened by extremist political groups which had arisen from the turmoil of the civil war. Acts of terrorism led first to the suspension of the constitution and a state of emergency, and then, in 1975, to the replacement of parliamentary by presidential government. Sheikh Mujib took dictatorial powers and his political party, the Bangladesh Peasants' and Workers' Awami League, was established as the only permitted political organization.

In August 1975 Mujib and his family were assassinated in an army coup. Khandakar Mushtaq Ahmed, a former Awami League leader, took over as president, declared martial law and banned all political parties. In November he was, in turn, overthrown by the army chief of staff, Brigadier Khalid Musharaf. He, in his turn, was ousted after four days and the government was taken over, jointly, by the heads of the three armed services, under a non-political president, the Chief Justice Abusadet Mohammad Sayem. Although political activities were allowed again in 1976, the elections planned for 1977 were postponed. In April 1977 General Zia ul-Rahman took over as president. The constitution was amended to emphasize the importance of Islam. In a national referendum 99 per cent of voters gave their support to the new president. An attempted coup in October 1977 was crushed and thirty service officers were executed. The three main political parties were then banned. Presidential elections in June 1978 resulted in a decisive victory for Zia. In December of that year martial law and censorship were ended in preparation for parliamentary elections. The elections, held in February 1979, passed off peacefully, although only 40 per cent of the electorate voted. President Zia's recently formed Bangladesh Nationalist Party won 207 of the 300 seats contested and a further 30 seats specifically reserved for women, although it only received 49 per cent of the votes cast. In April 1979 Bangladesh's re-admission to the Inter-Parliamentary Union signified the international acknowledgment that parliamentary government had at last been restored.

YOUNG HISTORIAN

A

1 What problems did partition create for Pakistan?

2 Why did East Pakistan break away to become Bangladesh?

3 Why has the political history of independent Pakistan been so troubled?

4 What difficulties does Bangladesh face in raising the living-standards of its people?

5 Find out how far Pakistan and Bangladesh have given more influence to Islam in recent years.

6 Explain the meaning of (a) autonomy, (b) "basic democracy", (c) legislature, (d) para-military, (e) "personality cult", (f) guerillas, (g) separatist, (h) ballot-rigging.

B

Write a dialogue in which one speaker supports a system of strong presidential rule for a developing country and the other supports a system of parliamentary government.

C

Write a series of headlines outlining the history of either Pakistan or Bangladesh since independence.

D

Draw a map of Pakistan and Bangladesh, showing the location of the major cities and rivers.

DATE LIST

1857	East India Company army rebellion. End of Mughal empire.
1858	Government of India taken over by the British Crown.
1869	Birth of Gandhi.
1877	Queen Victoria becomes Empress of India.
1885	First meeting of Indian National Congress.
1889	Birth of Nehru.
1905	Partition of Bengal.
1906	Formation of Muslim League.
1909	Morley-Minto reforms.
1911	Delhi Durbar, George V visits India.
1912	Capital moved from Calcutta to New Delhi.
1914	Gandhi returns to India from South Africa.
1919	Rowlatt Acts. Amritsar massacre. Montagu-Chelmsford reforms.
1920	Gandhi launches first civil disobedience movement.
1928	Simon Commission visits India.
1930	Gandhi's "Salt March". First Round Table Conference.
1931	Gandhi visits England.
1935	Government of India Act.
1937	Congress victories in provincial elections.
1939	Resignation of Congress ministries.
1940	Muslim League calls for a separate Pakistan.
1942	Cripps mission. "Quit India" movement.
1947	Independence and partition of India and Pakistan.
1948	Assassination of Gandhi. Death of Jinnah.
1950	Indian constitution comes into force.
1951	India launches first Five Year Plan.
1955	Nehru attends Bandung Conference of non-aligned nations.
1956	States Reorganization Act.
1958	Ayub Khan becomes President of Pakistan.
1960	"Basic democracy" inaugurated in Pakistan.
1961	India annexes Goa.
1962	War between India and China.
1964	Death of Nehru.
1965	War between India and Pakistan.
1966	Death of Lal Bahadur Shastri. Mrs Gandhi becomes Prime Minister.

1967	"Green Revolution" begins.
1969	Yahya Khan becomes President of Pakistan.
1971	Indo-Soviet Friendship Treaty. Independence of Bangladesh.
1972	Pakistan withdraws from Commonwealth.
1974	India explodes her first nuclear device.
1975	Declaration of Emergency by Mrs Gandhi. Assassination of Sheikh Mujibur Rahman.
1977	Mrs Gandhi defeated at general election.
1979	Execution of Zulfikar Ali Bhutto.
1980	Mrs Gandhi returned to power at general election. Death of Sanjay Gandhi.

BOOKS FOR FURTHER READING

Jean Bothwell, *The First Book of India* (Franklin Watts)
Evan Charlton, *India: Towards Independence* (Macmillan)
Michael Edwardes, *Nehru: a pictorial biography* (Thames & Hudson)
D. Judd, *The British Raj* (Wayland)
Elizabeth Katz, *India in Pictures* (Sterling)
Hyman Kublin, *India* (Houghton Mifflin)
Blaise Levai, *Ask an Indian about India* (Friendship Press)
Zaidee Lindsay, *India* (A & C Black)
Edward Rice, *Mother India's Children* (Friendship Press)
F.W. Rowding, *The Rebellion in India, 1857* (Cambridge University Press)
Percival Spear, *A History of India Vol. 2* (Penguin)
D.W. Sylvester, *Clive in India* (Longmans)
Natasha Talyarkhan, *India: the land and its people* (Macdonald Educational)
Jon A. Teta, *Pakistan in Pictures* (Sterling)
Charlotte Waterlow, *India* (Ginn)
Francis Watson, *Gandhi* (Oxford University Press)
Taya Zinkin, *India & her Neighbours* (Oxford University Press)

INDEX

The numbers in **bold type** refer to the figure numbers of the illustrations

and Round Table
    conferences 36
  since independence 83

Narayan, J.P. 60
nationalism, Indian 5-6,
  8, 19, 22, 25, 51
National Liberal
  Federation 28, 30, 36
Nehru, Jawaharlal 26, **33,
34, 35**
  and British rule 35, 37
  and Congress 56, 57
  early life 56
  and Gandhi 33, 51, 58
  as prime minister 58-9,
    62, 68, 74
  and Soviet Union 57, 74
Nehru, Motilal 35, 56
Nepal 72
newspapers, and politics 22,
  23, 26, 52; **29, 30**
Nobel Prize 25
non-alignment 68
nuclear programme, Indian
  6, 56, 68

Ottoman Empire 22, 27, 32

Pakistan
  constitution of 82-3, 84

creation of 41, 45-7, 82-3
economic development of
  89-90
leaders since inde-
  pendence 83-9; **51, 53,
54, 55**
place of Islam in 41, 83,
  88-9; **56**
and princely states 60
relations with India 56,
  69-71, 72
Pakistan People's Party
  (PPP) 86-7; **54**
"panchayat raj" 54
partition 45-7, 82; **26, 27**
population growth 64, 80,
  90
poverty 16, 54, 56, 62, 74,
  80, 86, 90; **6, 37**
princely states 14, 36-7, 60
Punjab 27, 28, 45-7, 62, 71,
  78, 80
"Pushtunistan" 83, 87

"Quit India" movement 42

railways 13, 16, 19, 35, 74,
  82-13, 17
Rajagopalacharian, C.R. 56
Ram, Jagjivan 64
Rann of Kutch 69, 71

refugees 47, 71, 82
riots 33, 45, 48, 52, 82, 86;
  27, 50
Round Table conferences
  35-7; **24**
Rowlatt Acts 28, 34
Ruskin, John 51
Russia, Tsarist 22, 25

"Salt March" 35-6; **23**
satyagraha 51
Second World War 41-2
Sèvres, Treaty of 32
Shah Commission 66
Shastri, Lal Bahadur 60
Sikkim 72
Simla 14, 42
Simon Commission 34-5, 37,
  42; **22**
Singh, Charan 66
South Africa, *see under*
  Gandhi, Mohandas
  Karamchand
Sri Lanka 72; **51**
State of Emergency 64
States Re-organization
  Commission 60
steel industry, Indian 19,
  73, 74; **43**
Suez Canal 19
swadeshi 23; **21, 32**

Swaraj party 34

Tagore, Rabindranath 25,
  51
Taj Mahal **1**
tariffs 22, 34
terrorism 23, 24, 28, 56, 90
Tibet 72
Tilak, B.G. 22, 24, 26, 27, 3
Tolstoy, Leo 51
"tribals" 6
"twenty-two families" 86

unemployment 54, 77, 80,
  90; **44, 46**
United Nations 68, 69, 71
universities, Indian 19, 22
"untouchables", *see* harijans
USA 23, 68, 71, 72
USSR 42, 57, 68, 71, 73, 74

Viceroy 14-15, 37; **15**
Victoria, Queen 16; **9**

Wavell, Lord 42
Willington, Lord 36
Wilson, President Woodrow
  27

Zia ul-Haq, General 87-9;
  55
Zia ul-Rahman, General
  90-1